For four years Lee Ly̲... ...LE AMAZON TRAIL has been .... lesbian and gay papers from coast to coast. Now, at last, it is available to her wide audience of lesbian readers who have been following her work in TOOTHPICK HOUSE, OLD DYKE TALES, THE SWASHBUCKLER, HOME IN YOUR HANDS and her latest novel, DUSTY'S QUEEN OF HEARTS DINER.

Lee covers the lesbian and gay scene from coast to coat, from inside our bookstores to inside our bars, from campfire to coven to careers, into and out of love. Growing up lesbian and being openly and proudly lesbian for thirty years and the rich perspective that comes from "The Good Life"; just one of the many sections of this delightful, sobering, fascinating and enriching collection.

Follow Lee from "The Good Life" through "Gay Lit," "Portraits," "Gay Rites" and "The Geography of Gay," into adventures as diverse as the secret haunts of famous writers to the food dubbed "Lesbian Stew" recommended for the temporarily bereft, from exploration of a notorious bar to learning to live soberly.

Lee tells us "Gay children flare up everywhere, stronger than religion and law and violence" and that "I wanted to spend my life writing from my heart in a way that will enhance the lives of my readers."

Take this journey with Lee along THE AMAZON TRAIL.

THE AMAZON TRAIL

by
LEE LYNCH

Withdrawn

the NAIAD PRESS inc.
1988

Printed in the United States of America
First Edition

Cover design and photograph of the author by Tee A.
Corinne

Cover drawing by Rupert Kinnard used with the
permission of *Just Out,* P.O. Box 15117, Portland,
Oregon, 97215.

Some of the essays in this book appeared in a limited
edition volume, THE AMAZON TRAIL, Grants Pass,
Oregon, Variant Press, 1986.

Library of Congress Cataloging-in-Publication Data

Lynch, Lee, 1945—
      The Amazon trail.

    1. Lynch, Lee, 1945   . 2. Lesbians--United
States--Biography. 3. Women authors, American--
Biography. 4. Lesbians--United States--Social
conditions. 5. Lesbians--United States--Intellectual
life. I. Title.
HQ75.4.L96A3 1988   306.7'663'0924   88-25350
ISBN 0-941483-27-4

Lee Lynch's column, *The Amazon Trail,* appears in the following publications:

Au Courant
Bay Area Women's News
Chicago Outlines
The Dallas Voice
ETC. Magazine
Just Out
The Lesbian News
Mama Bears News and Notes
Phoenix Resource
The Washington Blade

Lee Lynch is a member of the Gay and Lesbian Press Association.

For Tee Corinne,
who told me I could.

Special thanks to:
Tangren Alexander (Pearl Time's Child) for her
enthusiasm;
Norma Coleman, my good friend; Jay Brown and
Don Michaels for their fpatient editing, and
Renée LaChance for her support.

TABLE OF CONTENTS

THE GOOD LIFE

Becoming Her

Thirty years of being gay. Such a solid chunk of time is nothing to be sneezed at. If it were not for the dangers involved in marking our milestones by, for example, wearing five, ten, fifty year pins —

"What a lovely pin! A pink triangle with a seventy-five? Have you been *married* seventy-five years?"

"I , uh, well, not exactly. That is — I've been *gay* for . . . " No one wants to celebrate by watching horrified inquirers run screaming in the other direction.

Still, *I've* felt the urge to celebrate. With something like that in mind I mentioned this anniversary to my first lover, Suzy. We ended up in a friendly squabble about what year it actually had been. *I* said 1960, *Suzy* said 1959. I wanted her to be right. Coming out post-1970 makes one a woman's movement dyke in some circles; pre-1970 makes you "old gay." Discovering "the good life" before 1960 would have made Suzy and I part of a whole other, somehow more prestigious, era.

But 1960 it was. We were newly high school students, or had Suzy, too rebellious to fit in, too outspoken to hide, dropped out by then? I've forgotten a lot, but I remember a lot, too.

Like back streets. It seems we were always seeking the less populous back streets of New York where we could hold hands or dress up. One day Suzy came by the high school for me. Who knows how I got out early. How I dared to go into the girls' room and dress like I did. The clothes were boys', I remember that, and my hair was slicked back. I may have worn a tie, carefully covered by a fully zipped jacket. Thus I was transformed from a skinny, painfully introverted intellectual kid, into a swaggering, proud, fifteen year old butch, torn between wanting to be seen by my teachers, and needing to fade into the shaded back streets lined with curtained older homes. Suzy was likely to have been heavily made up, high-heeled (she was already three inches taller than me, damn her), in some sultry black outfit beneath which her stockinged legs flashed. I would have lit her Marlboro, then my own Kool as we, frightened but defiant, self-conscious but proud, made our way under the sheltering trees to the bus which would carry us where we wouldn't be known.

Were those the good old days? Sometimes they feel that way. I remember the loneliness, though. The only gay

4

we knew at first was an older woman all of eighteen who'd threatened to wait outside my school and beat me up for "taking Suzy away" from her. I have no idea if she ever showed — I hit the back streets and would go home the very long way.

In my senior year we finally made lesbian friends — Pete and Little Suzy. I'd fallen in love with Big Suzy, as she came to be called, while ice skating at an indoor rink. Something about the circumscribed circling, the grace of gliding on ice, the romantic organ music, even the hot dogs heaped with mustard, set my adolescent heart pounding. Suzy was warm and laughing in her soft furry jacket. I fancied myself graceful and dashing on the ice. Skating became part of our landscape of love.

It was on an outdoor pond that we met these first friends. We'd seen Pete back in junior high. Called Pat then, she'd been aloof and alone in the long cold corridors. We could not have named her attraction for us. Now, like a miracle, she reappeared. She was sixteen, handsome, tough, and had a girl of her own.

Awkwardly, shyly, we'd all meet, skate, share what we'd learned of the gay life. The ice on the pond eventually melted, but I recall a painful longing to love those two kids, and an equally painful reticence between us. We each tried so hard to be cool in our fledgling gay ways, that we couldn't say how glad we were to have peers. I felt practically normal as we double-dated, flirted, wove fantasies around one another, conjectured about the big gay world in which we yearned to find our places.

How Suzy and I strove to learn the ways of that world! Every chance we got, we'd be in Greenwich Village, watching the crowds for lesbians. This one's diddy-bop, that one's DA, another's jean jacket. We copied the right ways to smoke, to smile, to give other women The Look. I

5

wonder if there's a course in Signaling at the first official gay high school now located in the Village.

It was the unexpected, though, that always hit me hardest. I was a yearbook editor, along with my more exciting extra-curricular activities, and the whole editorial staff went into Manhattan one day to consult with the publisher. I was already writing, and the word "publisher" was to me what "Broadway" would be to an actress. Glamour colored the crowded office. I didn't care that the walls were lined with yearbooks instead of novels, technical journals instead of pretty volumes of poetry.

So when *She* walked in, I saw my future. She might have been an editor or a secretary, an artist or switchboard operator. This slight, dapper woman with short salt-and-pepper hair and the plain stamp of lesbian in every line of her face, every move of her body, was In Publishing. Oh my, she was perfect. While the yearbook staff poured over types and papers, I stole impassioned glimpses of Her. Hoped for a chance to give her The Look. Dressed her, in my mind, in street clothes, furnished her apartment, fixed her up with a bevy of femmes — no, with a long-term lover just like Suzy — no, with a cute young protege still in high school. She never noticed me.

Suzy watched as I graduated from high school that June. The next September, after two weeks at a faraway college, and an encouraging grade on my first English paper, I packed a small suitcase with underwear, clean shirts and innumerable books, tucked my portable typewriter under my arm, and ran away. I could wait no longer to become Her.

But as always, the main avenues were off limits. I got sidetracked onto the circuitous back streets and learned patience. I never saw Her again, never moved back to New

6

York. I broke up with Suzy in pursuit of fresh and varied pastures, lost touch with Pete, finished college like I was told to and stopped writing.

I didn't stop being gay, though. I became more and more a part of the subculture I'd studied with such devotion in those early years. I became, too, a part of the world of publishing. And — I'm reminded each time I pass a mirror and note the slight, dapper woman with short salt-and-pepper hair and the plain stamp of lesbian in every line of her face, every move of her body — I've become Her at last, the future I chose thirty years ago.

Cravat Caveat

I love wearing ties. If I had the money, I'd probably dress like something out of *GQ*. Girlfriend is delighted when I wear my brown leather flight jacket and tweed snap-brim cap. She responds by scheduling photo sessions with me — and in other more immediately gratifying ways.

I, in turn, am delighted when she gussies herself up in long skirts and exotic tops, adds a dash of eye enhancer and a dab of perfume. Now and then she'll even slip on a silky nightgown and a come-hither look, both of which affect me rather radically.

Or is *radical* the wrong word to use in these days when ultra-political crusaders attempt to "radicalize" us laggards by slashing at butch/femme behavior. I am tired of reading that butch/femme is an S and M *modus vivendi*. I am not a sadist or a masochist; neither is Girlfriend. I am not particularly aggressive in any aspect of my life; she is not particularly passive. Taking power frightens me; so does giving it up. I find romance, intellect and gentleness exciting. Like any pussycat, I can do tricks on my back and still land on all fours.

For me, femme/butch is a little bit about costuming, a little bit about posing, and a lot about who and what I find attractive. It's good clean fun.

After reading yet another diatribe by a writer who doesn't seem terribly well-informed about real-life lesbians, despite all her "research," I was angry enough to speak with a veteran. I called Frenchy Tonneau in Greenwich Village.

Now, Frenchy has changed some since her debut in *The Swashbuckler*. She's on her own again, but she and her ex, Mercedes, are great pals. Instead of haunting the bars, Frenchy is involved in preserving Village landmarks. She's also assistant manager of a local grocery store, and at the moment she spends most of her free time with three friends who have AIDS.

So, when I called to ask her reaction to the diatribe I'd sent her, I heard in her tone that she could hardly be bothered.

"Why doesn't she go back to men if she's so scared of real dykes?" Frenchy asked.

I laughed. Here I was ready to sound off about the insulting way the writer had attempted, like so many early women's movement "thinkers," to tell me how to be what I am perfectly naturally, a lesbian. Frenchy put her in perspective in one fell swoop.

I think Frenchy struck pay dirt, too, when she used the word *fear*. My perverse desire to wear a tie (which I'm using as a symbol of the butch stance) frightens people, both straight and gay. It seems to stir up some primeval muck inside that some can't handle.

In the olden days, that is, the early '70s, I felt a lot of disapproval when I indulged in my modified drag style. I agonized over going to a party — a dyke party — in clothes that felt dressed up to me. I knew I risked not being spoken to by many of the woman and having to fend off others. The androgyne is always a target — whether of derision or admiration or disgust. And a butch is always part androgyne, whether you can see it or only sense it.

But the fancy words are beside the point. I enjoyed dyking myself out. I'd had little occasion to do so in the past. First, because the word on the streets of New York was that one could be arrested for cross-dressing. Later, because I was shy and in an isolated relationship, so there was no place I could dress up except at home. Now the revolution was here. Women gathered in hordes all over New Haven, New York, everywhere. We were no longer bound by social codes that regulated everything from who we loved to how we dressed. Or so I thought until I put on my ties. There were discussions about trying to be like men. About scaring away the straight women. My tie collection grew. Many of the tie bashers eventually returned to heterosexual relationships. Or closets.

These days, Girlfriend and I wear the various costumes which explore, display and exhibit our selves. If I stand, legs apart, pelvis forward, hands outspread at pocket level — a perfectly natural position for me —

Girlfriend will jump me, but other women will be scared, embarrassed or ashamed and will call our behavior something nasty . . . like "role-playing."

Is butch/femme role-playing? Sure, it's an acting out. At its most extreme it can mean adoption of rigid behaviors — kind of like being politically; correct can lead to a similar rigidity. *I* love to diddy-bop into a room, hitch up my pants, roll up my sleeves and start to crochet. I love to come home and find Girlfriend going at a board with the electric saw which scares me to death.

I pressed Frenchy further for her comments on the diatribe.

"Listen, kid," she went on. Frenchy is six years older than me, 48 now. "One of the things I like about you is, you might be a writer, but you don't jump on any bandwagon. You talk about stuff you know. This one, it's none of her business how we conduct ourselves. I've met plenty like her, too. There's a shitload of them since the libbers started coming around. I don't know what they turn on to — maybe doing it in the mud at those music festivals — and that's OK. Just stay off my turf."

"What would you say butch/femme is about, Frenchy?"

"Hell, what do I know? That's like asking what real life is about when you're a kid. You have to kind of feel your way." She chuckled at her play on words.

"No, seriously," I urged. "You're the expert."

"Me? An expert?" Frenchy said, feigning modesty. Briefly. "You know, you're right. If there's one thing I'm an expert at, it's being gay. But you know who else is an expert is my best drag-queen friend Mary-Mary Q. Contrary. *She* sees life as — what does she call it? — a courting ritual. Everybody has their own steps. Maybe some men are born nellie. Maybe some women end up

11

aping somebody they like: their dads, their moms, their Uncle Bert. It doesn't really matter, is what Mary-Mary says, as long as you're dancing to your own tune."

I was beginning to feel better. Not just one, but two experts were saying it's OK to be me and to be angry at a sister pervert who wants to feel less perverted than me.

"OK," I said, "now I know what Mary-Mary thinks. What about Frenchy?"

She was silent for a long moment. "Butch," she finally declared, "is knowing how to stand on a streetcorner and catch a femme's eye."

"And femme?"

"Is spotting the butch and knowing how to get her clothes off."

"But, Frenchy," I said, laughing. "I thought we were talking equality here. Are you saying the femme is the active partner?"

She chuckled again. "Don't you *know* that by now?"

The Amazon Trail

Moving down Mt. Sexton out of a sea of clouds and fog, under, incredibly, a rainbow, into this sun-filled, wildflower-strewn valley that first time — I should have known I was coming home. But it took a few more days. It took till our hostesses Tee Corinne and her lover drove for hours to show us Crater Lake. Well, I said, noting silently that Cape Cod had nothing on this incredible volcanic lake, maybe I'd be willing to talk about moving here. Maybe.

That was in June, 1982. I had been working in the Naiad Press booth at the National Women's Studies Conference in Arcata, California. Rosemary Curb, co-editor of *Lesbian Nuns*, and Chris Czernik of the Boston Lesbian and Gay History Project were also guests in that crowded household. One night, Tee made several phone calls and out of those apparently uninhabited mountains of Southern Oregon swarmed more dykes than I would see in my first *month* back in New Haven, Connecticut. Chris presented her slide show, I read in public for the first time, and Hannah Blue Heron played her fiddle. The group was as exciting and as welcoming as the mountains themselves. Had I stumbled upon a veritable lesbian Mecca? Or should I say Lesbos . . .

Just in case, I moved to Southern Oregon in March of 1984.

"Watch out," warned my friend Taz, calling from her snowed-in suburban house in Connecticut to make sure *I* was all right. "Don't get involved in any of that *weird* stuff out there. That *witchcraft.*"

"I may not drink any more, Taz," I replied, "or smoke, or eat white sugar. But I'm here for the mountains and the culture, not women's spirituality." At least, not for anything *weird*. I'd been to Rootworks and the women there were transplanted Easterners like myself. How could I explain it to her? How just looking through, breathing in, the Southern Oregon air had so bewitched Deb and I we'd packed up a condominium-by-the-sea full of furniture and cats and shipped all of our dreamy-eyed selves three thousand miles westward. Taz' skepticism reminded me of my own reluctant joy in the land.

But she was, in a sense, right to warn me that behind the rainbows that festoon the rainy/sunny skies, it would be hard here. My acre and a half empire is incredibly

14

demanding. I shudder when the rains come raging through the creek threatening to take with them my already rickety bridges. The distances I travel to buy a Sunday paper or a bagel, to earn a buck, would have seemed impossible to me back East. The brilliant white cast of summer light, the sense of these solid-hearted mountains sitting out the centuries long before me, long after me, have pulled me up sharp, turned me around, forced me to reassess my hasty, compartmentalized Eastern life —

And now I'm here on my own, in training to be a rugged, independent Oregonian. Living, but for Girlfriend next door, alone in the woods like a back-to-the-women's-land collectivist with all the conveniences. Nights, I walk down a pitch-black fog-shrouded country road where werewolves, for goodness sake, could get me, according to the late night movies I was raised on in New York City. Hauling wet wood, mending the barn roof (from the inside — it was raining), growing all seven tomatoes in my first-ever garden — it's all so new and hard.

But, I tell Taz in letters, it's not at all weird. It feels so natural and I'm so changed with the change in lands.

I've learned how to burn wet wood. I've blazed my own trail up to Mother Kali's Bookstore in Eugene and found as fine a feminist bookstore as any in Connecticut. Ashland is about as far from me as New York City was, but the freeway is a joy to drive compared to Bruckner Boulevard and Bloomsbury Books, in Ashland, carries lesbian novels. You can go to good — and bad — theatre year round, including Tennessee Williams' apparently lesbian play "Something Unspoken," in a recent fantastic production. Then there's the Southern Oregon Women's Writers Group, Gourmet Eating Society and Chorus.

15

Despite Taz' fear that my writing style would change radically out here, I found this group, so unique to Southern Oregon, was just what I needed.

And look at them! At Hannah Blue Heron whose musical fantasy "From the Other Side of Madness" was performed at the Northwest Women's Cultural Festival in Olympia, Washington last year. At Tangren Pearl Time's Child who self-published a fascinating book called *The Auto Biography of Deborah Carr.* At Tee Corinne, her art, her books. At Ruth Mountaingrove, who created with Jean *Womanspirit Magazine* and is still a fountain of poetry and songs and photography. I look at these core group members and thank the mountains for welcoming me so grandly.

It's the Amazon Trail, then, I'm traveling and writing about. Every dyke has found at least a bit of it. For some it leads only as far as the nearest gay bar. Others have criss-crossed the country, the world, connecting with other lesbians along the way. For me, today, it's the I-5 corridor from L.A. to Vancouver. Tomorrow — who knows?

Lesbian Economics

Once upon a time, not so long ago, a group of fifteen women sat before a woodstove in Southern Oregon, rain incessant but comforting outside, and talked. Noticeable was a lack of controversy, criticism, and bitterness. Newly present were evidence of foresight, a confrontation with real problems and a recognition of the enemy as outsider, rather than among us.

"Carol and me," said Danna in her slow, seemingly casual voice, "we've been working our asses off building. We want to start our bed and breakfast this spring."

"Can you make a living from one of those?"

"No. But I want to be a farmer. It'll supplement the farm."

A professional counselor across the room suggested, "Lesbians make money. We need ways to spend it on other lesbians' goods and services."

Sue, soft-spoken, with lively blue eyes, is the new owner of a small grocery store in Grants Pass. "It's a question of economic survival these days."

"Yeah," agreed several women.

"After five years, we're still operating our health food store out of love," said Daphne from It's a Natural on Second Avenue in Myrtle Creek. "It's gotten to the point, though, where Judith is considering taking a job."

"Still," offered Judith with enthusiasm, "once we were 'those people up there.' Now the community welcomes our presence in projects."

The artist of the group was offering her work for sale that day. "I'm trying to support myself partially with my art. This is where you come in," she said to us all, gesturing toward a wide variety of possible Christmas gifts. "I need to know what you want. That will help to shape what I do."

I, too, have dealt with this question of survival. My books earn back only my expenses — for which I'm grateful. But I support myself with a straight job. Last night I dreamt a whole beginning-to-end spy novel with a lesbian heroine. I woke thinking, "*This* is how I'll make enough money to write full time!" Then I thought, "Is this how I want to spend the next two years of my life? Violence, fear — Super-Sappho saving the world?" I may

18

have to consider it after I fail to get any of the grants or awards I've applied for from the straight world. I may have to if I give up on getting concrete support from our gay culture.

Why don't I make money from my books? The lesbian market is just beginning to be visible, reachable. Lesbians don't have or won't spend their money on books. I can't be awarded (even if I deserved them) a Gay Guggenheim, a Perverts' Pulitzer, when neither exists yet. And they won't exist until we see ourselves as a group which deserves mutual support.

Sue's living on the edge, along with Daphne, Judith and the farm-hoteliers, partly because we're just beginning to mature as a culture, just beginning to recognize our responsibility for and to ourselves economically. When we were kids it was okay to live in student ghettos, eat fast food diets, work minimum wage jobs, squander our safety, health and energies. But now?

I once sat in rag-tag circles of theorists, complaining about the patriarchy. I once applauded the spray-painting sloganeers, took over a radio station, lived on unemployment, alcohol and drugs. I've also worked full-time, owned my home and established good credit.

The women around the woodstove were saying that they, too, had not found solutions in separatism or in absorption into the mainstream. They wanted to be self-supporting and some want to specialize in serving women. Perhaps only the professional haircutter who was with us can do both right now.

The artist got a monetary show of support that day. The others began with the seed of a plan. Perhaps a brochure to be distributed in the lesbian community regionally, or even nationally. Dare we think of a lesbian Chamber of Commerce? The brochure would sport a map

of this Amazon Trail of ours, with lavender markers for
our own businesses and a listing of local highlights and
services along the way. Certainly ads in the local
alternative papers. A counter-culture, is, after all, a
culture, its media as real and potentially as effective as
any other.

A little thrill ran through me. As important as they
are, too, this was not a group considering means to
symbolically take back the night. This was not a group
considering whether it should censor S&M material. This
was not a group considering whether women should have
children, own pets, eat only vegetables, shave their legs.

"*We* don't want to be changing bedsheets for
straights," one of the farmers said strongly.

"We're glad to work with a whole community," was
the tone of the natural food sellers.

The grocer is always open-armed to the dykes who
travel out of their way to play Pacman or buy lunch in her
store. She loves her work, they all love their work, and
they're ready to balance profit and loss, know-how and
learning, caution and flagrant queerness, to be themselves
in a world of their own making.

In the next room was a tablefull of homemade foods.
The group re-formed around it, seemingly unchanged. But
were they a little stronger for sharing their vision? This
process of envisioning and building is so gradual. Look at
the centuries behind us, when such a group would not
have thought to meet, or had they met, might have been
arrested for witchcraft. Look at some of the surges of
woman-power before: the ancient amazons, the flagrant
lesbians of the twenties, the self-sufficient women of
World War II. There are those who say men took the
power in ancient times to control ownership of land. The
depression of 1929 seemed to put an end to that emerging

20

lesbian culture. When the men returned after World War II, the women passively handed over the reins.

Economics is obviously a key to winning back our place in the world — and to making a world of our own. What we craft now before our woodstoves, must be slow, considered, sound. We've always worked our asses off for someone else. Will we finally do it for each other?

A Place For Us: Gay Bars

A few weeks ago Girlfriend said, impetuously, enthusiastically, "I want to go to a gay bar!" I felt her urge throb in my veins, too. It had been a long time since I'd sat among my own people and watched our rites and mysteries unfold in a dim, smoke-filled room.

Not long after this we traveled to Eugene to hear Gerd Brantenberg read from *Egalia's Daughters,* and we joined the crowd that afterward dispersed, then regouped, at a bar affectionately called "The Riv," right in Eugene's downtown mall.

A new gay bar is always exciting to me, though so often the same as every other. This one was large, with a long bar at one side of an open space, and an equally large, if empty, dance floor on its other side. Blinking lights outlined the ceiling over the dance floor and seemed to pulse to the beat of loud, unintelligible music. There were a few tables across from the bar, as well as a pool table, and several dykes in wheelchairs conversed there with others on straight-backed chairs. We climbed some steps to overlook the scene from a raised platform which held still more tables.

It was a bare place, with nothing to decorate it but the patrons: women in baggy western casual, men in crisper togs. There was a smell of cigarette smoke everywhere. I tasted of it and nothing else for hours. Our voices grew hoarse with it and with the increasingly raucous music.

My visit led me to think of Bonnie Zimmerman's work. She's a teacher of lesbian literature and women's studies at the University of California. One theme she's identified in our books is the search for haven, for what she, along with Isabel Miller, calls *A Place For Us* (the original title of *Patience and Sarah*). I can't think of a truer example of life mirrored in literature.

Most young gay people, uncertain of their identities or goals, and rejecting arrangements the world has made for them, undertake such a search. But most young people, growing older, settle into the very worlds they've fled, or at most, stretch them, subtly rearrange them, till they can comfortably nest within — and without, before the eyes of the world.

Gay people — well, we may even relish the thought of adapting to the cozy old world of our families, of the

23

generations which have produced us, but we trip on the very doorstep that we'd enter. The most conservative of us — who look right, act right, move about without the telltale lover — carries her/his difference within. And that difference sometimes, somehow, will always flash inadvertently, when least expected, before the worst possible audience. I think back to Sherwood Anderson's story "Hands." The hands in the piece belong to a gay man, and betray him finally, because in them — their gestures, their energy, their form — he carried and expressed without design, all he was.

Where would such hands go unremarked except for their beauty? Where would Hall's Stephen Gordon dance without notice in her severe and masculine skirted suits? Where would Moll Cutpurse drink and brawl, fight over a femme with Beebo Brinker? Where would Patience and Sarah "melt" unobtrusively in a corner?

There is no place on earth we'd all fit but, drinkers or not, in a gay bar. And I suspect there is no place on earth one can wander without finding The Riv under a thousand different neon-lit names.

My first gay bar was called the Swing Rendezvous. The tradition that shortened the Riv's real title transformed mine to The Swing or The Swing-a-long. (And this liberty with given names is certainly a queer tradition.) The bar was in Greenwich Village, smack in the midst of the thriving folk scene where Bob Dylan and Joan Baez were beginning to attract national attention. Inside The Swing we knew little of all that.

This insular world of The Swing was much smaller, physically, than The Riv. Up some steps, you'd enter the barroom itself, with a juke box and an old wooden phone booth crammed along the opposite wall. I smoked then, so smelled only the perfumes of femmes, the hair tonic and

24

after shave of butches, the sting of spilled alcohol, the reek of beery breaths. It was a lesbian bar, for the most part, and the regulars, the cruisers, the strangers who stumbled in, perched on stools to watch new entries in the gold-flecked mirror behind the bar. A tiny back room was lined with tables, and offered a dance floor so tight you couldn't be sure who your partner was, unless the song was a slow one, and you were doing the "bump and grind." Doing it, that is, at least until the waitress with the impressive nickname "Chopsy" told you the bartender wanted you to stop. It was illegal to dance so close, or was it illegal to dance at all? Different bars seemed to interpret the laws differently. "D'youse," Chopsy would ask, "want the place closed down?" Heck, no. It was a place for *us*.

At the Music Box around the corner I was more likely to find a homogeneous, rather than a homosexual, mix. An interracial straight couple. Two older gay men. Some very young lesbian couples without I.D.'s darting looks shyly at everyone, like kids at the circus for the first time. Kids who'd been well trained to keep their enthusiasms under cover.

We didn't dance at the Box at all. The presence of straights inhibited us. This place was ours only in geography and ambiguity. Obviously they'd take anyone's money in hopes of catching on with some free-drinking crowd. We probably would have been safer dancing there, where they were as uncertain of their fortunes as we were of ours, and because it wouldn't be as much of a target for gay busts as a Swing. But we were young, we were alone in our wonderland (as Johnny Mathis assured us on every juke box), and we were students of The Good Life.

The Good Life. Another popular song back then was *The Good Life*, sung by Andy Williams. It was immediately adopted as a sweet-sour anthem by gays. How *The Good Life seemed to be the ideal.* How it *let you hide all the sadness you feel* . . . I always marvelled when I learned that the phrase The Life was shared with prostitutes. And I suspect used by both with the same defiant pride. The pride of outlaws claiming something of their own. Something difficult to name: "the love that dare not speak its name," in Radclyffe Halls' words.

Both groups were sexual outlaws: neither with a place of our own anywhere but the underside of society where, hidden by the shade of night and secrecy, those living in the light could and did visit, whether to vent their rage or take their pleasure, and then steal away. Steal our excitement, our strange confined freedom, then deny it and, doing so, enforce our denial, too.

Alone in our Wonderland. For twenty years I thought I, or the couple I was in, was the only one alone. That there was some connection between underworld people that kept me sitting at tables for two while they pushed a half-dozen together and still overflowed them. At The Riv last night I watched an isolated couple pretend not to watch the rest of us, bravely dance on an empty floor, elbow their way to the bar to order more, probably unwanted, drinks. They don't know yet what I so lately learned, that being alone is like being without a place. There is no one, nor is there anyplace, but what we take, or make, for ourselves.

History has given us the gay bars. Girlfriend's urge to visit one was a call of the blood. The Riv, The Swing-a-long, The Box, are rich with generations of our lives, and I'll always return, now and then, till there's another place for us where I can be with my own and get what I need.

The Notorious Ace of Spades

I miss a lot less about the East Coast than I thought I might. New York, yes, but that's my hometown. Being within walking distance of a store that sells the *Times* yes, but instead I'm surrounded by powerfully peaceful mountains which do a lot more for my well-being. Friends, definitely, but I'm such a hermit that I probably communicate better by mail anyway.

It's Provincetown that sometimes calls me back. Provincetown which comes flooding into my consciousness at odd times, a place that feels like lying in a lover's arms. Provincetown, Massachusetts, a site of easy memories and bright yellow days, and of my young, young, quest for myself.

Carol Lynne and I went that first time in, perhaps, 1969. Ours was a college marriage. When all the other girls got engaged, we became lovers. When they all graduated and had their weddings, we collected some cats and set up housekeeping in the ghetto. When they all flew off to Puerto Rico or the Virgin Islands for honeymoons we, somewhat belatedly, made our first timid foray into Provincetown. P-Town, as the veterans called it. Ah, to so comfortably belong!

We rented a motel room in North Truro, next door. I almost think we would have stayed there, in hiding, if we hadn't been forced into the Gay mecca to find food. Bellbottoms. I remember that we wore our very best, probably ironed, bellbottoms into the fray. I remember that painful mixture of staring/not staring which was cruising for us. The pinky signals with which we told each other, "There's one!"

Provincetown itself is pretty tacky. It's a tourist town. Because Gays flock there some of the touristy things are more interesting, but there were innumerable shops which specialized in plastic squeeze purses imprinted with Cape Cod, Mass.

We loved it. Bought the sweatshirts and T-shirts and hats and postcards that we, middle-class-state-employee-social-service types, would have bought anywhere. But back then, even before the concept of Gay culture had been hatched on any large scale, because we were Gay we were able to step into another level of experience. The straight tourists, secretly search as they might for the fascination of Gay life, could not enter this world. It was made of nuance, colored by need, and the directions were not on any Chamber of Commerce map.

I was familiar with the history of the place. We sat one night in terribly uncomfortable folding wooden chairs, backs to the harbor, feet on a sandy splintery wooden floor, and watched a tedious Eugene O'Neill production in a crowded firetrap called the Provincetown Playhouse. I am so grateful that I got there before the Playhouse disappeared for good. Djuna Barnes once sat in front of that stage, and Edna St. Vincent Millay, and many, many others, aspiring literary Gays like myself. It seemed every time I went searching for a biography of a suspected Gay writer they'd spent a summer, a winter, at Provincetown.

The bookstore. I can't recall its name, but on vacations I half-lived there. By my last trip in 1983, the shelves were packed with blatantly Gay literature. Back then, again, one had to know what one was looking for. *Giovanni's Room* was always prominent. Gore Vidal's books. Carson McCullers and Mary Renault and Truman Capote. The writers one suspected, just from their work, but couldn't be certain of. Yet. We wondered about the salespeople. I was writing for *The Ladder* at the time and much later learned that the woman who sat at the bookstore cash register was a *Ladder* cover artist, as anonymous as myself.

Were there drag shows back then? I don't remember. There certainly was not an influential Gay businessperson's group, nor were there openly Gay guesthouses, a Womancrafts store. There *was* Herring Cove Beach. Like a combined music festival and faerie gathering from the future, the beach was life-changing. Never before had I seen so many Gays in one place. It didn't matter a bit if I talked to anyone or anyone to me, we were all still scared of one another and shy, still raw from the rejection of the rest of the world. They were there, an incontestable fact, in the biggest, broadest, brightest sunlight they could find. And I was surrounded for once by my own.

One night Carol and I put on our very best ironed bellbottoms and strolled the town with the nonchalance of carefree window shoppers. Our disguise did not fool us. Hearts hammering, we were looking for the notorious Ace of Spades, the Lesbian bar.

Now remember, back then the word Lesbian had a sinister cast. The word bar doubled it. I'd been hearing about the Ace of Spades since age fifteen. By 1969 I'd built it in my head into a towering dungeon-like affair frequented by knife-wielding, duck-tailed, leather-jacketed, burly half-women who snarled at their slight, teased-haired femmes and laughed four-eyed, college-educated, scrawny baby-butches like me off the face of the earth.

Carol and I finally ran out of shops to linger in. The Ace of Spades was up toward the end of the earth — that is, the end of town. To get to it, we turned down a long dark narrow alley. The bar was built out over the beach. The alley smelled of salty fog and felt as clammy as my hands. It was empty, but we could hear music pound inside the walls of the bar. It was all I could do not to tiptoe. There was nothing on earth I wanted so much as to be in that bar, to join in The Gay Life — nothing except to run like hell. We approached. Lacking the nerve to go through the door, I craned my neck to peer in one of those windows. I did not recover from the shock of what I saw for years.

Inside this towering dungeon-like affair were knife-wielding, duck-tailed, leather-jacketed burly half-women snarling at their slight, teased-haired femmes and

30

laughing this four-eyed, college-educated, scrawny baby butch off the face of the earth. We turned tail and scurried back to the bright straight lights.

Was that really what I saw? Or did I have in that moment nothing but a glimpse of my own fears, a vision of who the world predicted, and I feared, I would become?

When I next went back, a few years later, the bar had changed hands and was called The Pied Piper. The tremors of Stonewall, the tentacles of the women's movement, had reached Provincetown. And me. When I looked inside myself now, the Lesbian I saw was not an Ace of Spades at all. She was a Pied Piper. This time, when I went down that long Provincetown alley, I opened the door and went in.

Living Sober: San Francisco

Those who've been lucky enough to visit San Francisco know the feel of a sunny summer day like no other. The breeze off the water has a tang to it that's soothed by a bleached white sun you'd close your eyes against if you could bear to shut out the sight of the city it beautifies. Or the people it reveals. The amazing and omnipresent and aggressively alive gay people.

They were arriving from all over the country when I reached the Civic Center, Thursday, the second of July.

By Saturday the workshops would overflow, the hallways would teem, the auditoriums would fill. These were a special breed of gay people, sober, clean, refusing to help one another be anything but all we could be.

I felt like the butterfly of the Living Sober logo: I flitted from Alcoholics Anonymous to Al Anon to Adult Children of Alcoholics meetings. I've been active in one or another of these for three years now, but never felt so at home, so understood and reflected. We'd all tried, with our addiction of choice, to nullify our existence. We spent years *blottoed, blitzed, smashed, stoned, bombed* and all the other ironically apt words that describe the violent lemming-like self-destruction which kept/keeps us from realizing our full potential. Which makes it so easy for gay people to ignore the ways in which we've learned to blot, blitz, stone and bomb ourselves for being who we are.

Silly, aren't we? The straight world says we hate you, you're no good, go away, we want to KILL YOU ALL. And we feed ourselves the subtle liquids, powders and weeds which are toxic to so many of us. These substances may not kill us directly, but absorb who we are so thoroughly that the slow suicide they induce becomes less painful than any state of full being. For those who don't like the feel or taste of intoxicants, why they can choose a partner or a job with whom they can become so obsessed they too *wipe out* themselves.

THE WORKSHOPS (chaired by one man, one woman) tell their own stories — The Long Road Home From Self-Loathing, To Self Loving. You're Only As Sick As Your Secrets. Emotional Sobriety. Fear of Intimacy. Anonymous Sex In Sobriety. Reality Is Not Always the Place I Want To Be. So Your Friend Has AIDS. — I felt like I'd come home.

THE PROFESSIONAL RESOURCES — Mary Cavagnaro's A Double Dose of Denial — Growing Up Gay In An Alcoholic Family. Liz Nadoff and Nan Jervey's Violence and Battery In Lesbian Relationships. Richard T. Clinton's Nutrition and Recovery. — Talking about my life, what a miracle.

THE SPEAKERS — A young boy from Al-Ateen, talking about growing up in an alcoholic lesbian household, black, too young for any support group, and how he learned to survive. Two men, alcoholics, both with AIDS, so grateful for the AA program in which they are learning to live fully even while staring into the face of their own mortality. Ex bar dykes, freeing themselves of compulsive addictions and sex, amazed at their accomplishments now that they have had time and energy for other things.

THE ENTERTAINMENT — Where but San Francisco would an amateur musical measure up to much I've seen professionally? Funny and moving, its saddest point for me was the music of Michael Bennett's *Chorus Line*, adapted to the show. Bennett had died the day before — of AIDS.

MY EXPERIENCE — I left for a while Saturday afternoon because I'd also come to the city to gather material for a book. I wandered around and happened onto the Haight-Noriega bus, having no idea where I was going. Within two minutes an older dyke from Living Sober had introduced herself to me. We immediately named our mutual friends — found ourselves related in the gay family. But I was aware while we talked of an unsettled feeling and a queasiness in my stomach. I wished I had a teddy bear.

Teddy bears were one of the commemorative items being sold. At least half the participants must have bought bears to hug and hold and rock in comfort as their own pain surfaced in workshops and meetings. *I*, however, had long ago given up relating to stuffed animals. I have my cats, after all, my lover. I'm a grown-up, aren't I?

My new friend reached her stop and left me alone. The bus plunged on through the hippie-punky-lefty Haight crowds, west toward The Great Highway and the Pacific Ocean, into such stark white sunlight it seemed every detail of the streets and houses and people would be revealed.

Like me. Living sober, the twelve step programs, are my searchlight. I'd just been through days of being totally revealed to myself. Now I sat, utterly alone, in such emotional pain I felt physically ill and clutched my stomach like the walking wounded, for comfort, for safety, to keep my guts from spilling out. What could I do to ease my own pain?

I walked along the beach, soothing myself with the sight of the ocean, the feel of the healing sun, the delicate hardiness of the wildflowers. In a flash I understood why all those people back at the roundup carried teddy bears. They were holding onto them for dear life. Did I really need to be unique? A teddy bear would be salve for my wounds. Was I too full of pride to carry a bear and reveal that I suffered, too?

This time when the bus reached Haight Street I got off and went into a trendy toy store. They had a very large selection of bears. I searched and worried for an hour till I settled on my bear. I named her Easy. Because it's not. Not one bit.

That night Easy came with me, in her thrift-store lavender tie, to the big AA meeting in the Main Auditorium. It was countdown night. The Chairs called

35

for everyone one day sober to stand up. A few people rose and received enthusiastic applause for their accomplishment. Thirty days was called, then sixty, then ninety. One year. Six years (Easy and I stood proudly in this group). Twenty, thirty, thirty-six years!

I can't think of a moment in my life more fulfilling than that night, when, amidst all the standing and cheering and applause, the Chairs announced that there were four thousand of us in that room. Four thousand lesbians and gay men willing to say we are too worthwhile to turn weapons on ourselves any more. Willing to face the revealing, healing, beautifying, life-giving sunlight we turn on each other. I clutched my bear and joined in the crowd's roar.

GAY LIT

Gay Press Row: The American Booksellers Association Convention

I'm at the Portland, Oregon stop on the Amazon Trail, penning this column about my visit May 23 and 24 to the ABA. Wondering why everything always happens at once, as I'm at the airport, waiting for my flight to the National Women's Music Festival in Indiana. But that's another column.

Moscone Center, San Francisco. Picture an enclosed football stadium, minus bleachers, filled with books.

Filled with booth after booth of publishers large and small, filled with bookstore owners, authors, salespeople, posters, gimmicks. A veritable carnival of the intellect. The only thing one couldn't do was aim rifles at a gallery full of right wing publishers.

Then picture a row about a quarter of a mile away from the start of your walk (and it's not even the last row). Notice the people milling about look — *different.* More casual, perhaps? Friendlier? More sincere? Is that a woman giving you THE LOOK? You've wandered into Gay Press Row! There's Alyson Publications at the end, with owner Sasha Alyson, tall, well-built, boyishly handsome in light pants, shirtsleeves, with his weathered, floppy-eared stuffed dog in his arms. Two assistants help him take orders for *The Hustler, Iris,* all their titles.

Next door, Firebrand, with Nancy K. Berreano at the helm, her lineless face always so lovely under that shock of grey hair. *Moll Cutpurse,* a lesbian picaresque novel, caught my eye, as did Pat Parker's *Jonestown and Other Madness.*

Beside her, Naiad Press, queen of them all, Donna McBride and Barbara Grier proudly selling, shooing away their Famous Authors to avoid a blockage of the aisles. Nancy Manahan and Rosemary Curb, looking fresh and fulfilled, but sounding, acting a little bleary and shook-up in the midst of their promotional tour. Tee Corinne, *Yantras of Womanlove;* Katherine Forrest, just finishing up *The Emergence of Green;* myself, with *The Swashbuckler* handsomely displayed beside *Sex Variant Women in Literature,* Jeanette Foster's classic study of lesbian writing.

Everywhere I turn I'm tripping over another author. Peg Cruikshank, *New Lesbian Writing* (Grayfox Press); Joyce Bright, reviewer and author; Jeff Black, an Alyson author; Janis Kelly, former *Off Our Backs* collective member.

Then came Knight, a gay male press rumoured to pay advances and in other ways actually treat writers as if writing is our profession, not a hobby. Then Seal Press, where author Barbara Wilson is selling her latest, *Murder in the Collective*. She and other Press members Rachael, Faith and Sally are working with translations from Scandinavian countries and Japan. One of the upcoming books is a comic novel about a place where women are dominant and men wear skirts.

After passing Feminist Bookstore Newsletter, Spinsters Ink, Cleis Press, Crossing Press, the Women in Print booth, Down There Press, Kitchen Table Press, Frog in the Well Press — how gratifying to swagger past Farrar Straus & Giroux, Harper and Row, Bantam, Penguin — and have a place in it all even if I am "only" a gay writer!

To back up, on the night of our arrival Girlfriend and I went directly to Raggs, a downtown San Francisco gay bar. This part of the festivities was sponsored by some of the lesbian and gay presses. There, I met such luminaries as Del Martin, full of the energy that's accomplished so much for lesbians. Phyllis Lyon was with her, lionesque, another early visionary. A new Naiad author and her lover, a Jungian therapist; Vivian and Pam from Pandora Books in Englewood, New Jersey; Joan Densmore and Dana Farmer from Rubyfruit Books in Tallahassee, Florida. Joan told me about the "straight" women who work for the Florida legislature. They stock up on lesbian books at her store while in town for each session!

Another story came from Donna McBride of Naiad. A lesbian ex-nun visited her local Waldenbooks and took *Lesbian Nuns* up to the counter. The salesperson said,

"You don't want to buy that book. It's disgusting!" The lesbian turned to the line of customers, waved the blatant gold-lettered title before them, and asked, "Does anyone *else* mind me buying this book?" One can hope the salesperson felt properly foolish.

I met one of our foremost gay researchers, Eric Garber, that night. Though he's worked on many projects, his long-lived passion is for the Harlem Renaissance. The lists of gays and bisexuals he reeled off! To think, my favorite blues singer! So many others unfortunately unnameable in print because they're still living. He was the one, too, who Barbara Grier called when she needed the last link in her search for author Gale Wilhelm. Naiad reprinted Wilhelm's exquisite *We Too Are Drifting* and *Torchlight to Valhalla,* but no one knew if Wilhelm was even alive. Thankfully, she's very much alive, though elderly and ill, and living with a lover on the west coast. How sad she hasn't known all these years how important she's been to so many. How grateful I am for Grier's diligence and resourcefulness.

I also spoke with Tede (pronounced Teddy) at the party. He is the drag queen in "Word Is Out," who was, as a passing friend commented, "in drag" for the party: tie and beard, narrow-lapel jacket, white shirt, black pants. He was transformed, but still cute, wise-eyed. I told him how I'd patterned my first male character, Starr, after him. Starr is important to me because he is a feminist male who recognizes and expresses his female side and lives in the world in a very womanly way. I told Tede it wasn't until after I'd seen "Word Is Out" a second time, after creating Starr, that I realized he'd been my model. Tede, who now works at Modern Times Bookstore in San Francisco and is a poet, seemed excited that he'd had such an impact on someone.

Tede also told a story. This one's about his mother, who knew he was gay, but hadn't been told he was a "hooker" or drag queen. He was worried about her reaction to these revelations in "Word Is Out" until she saw it and complained instead, "But, Tede, you said I was a *strong woman.* I couldn't help it. I had to be strong to raise kids in those days!" "But, Mom," answered Tede, "that's not an insult! Some of my best friends are strong women!"

I moved on to Susie Bright, editor of *On Our Backs,* a magazine of lesbian erotica which seeks to publish a wide range of sexual tastes and experiences. Honey Lee Cottrell was also there, a photographer often published in *On Our Backs* as well as other women's magazines, and the cover model for *The Swashbuckler.*

Kirio Spooner, founder of Womonfyre Books in Northhampton, Massachusetts, has moved south to work at Womanbooks in New York City. And was at ABA with Karyn London, Womanbooks owner, who'd brought the painful news that Sonny Wainwright had died. Sonny wrote *Stage V — A Journal Through Illness,* just published last year, and had recently retired from a position as assistant principal in the NYC public school system. A former phys ed teacher, Sonny was small, tough, a woman who contributed richly to our community.

From Raggs, a group of us went over to the Sheraton for a snack. I left the group to find the women's bathroom, completely unprepared for what I'd fine in there. Girls. Girls at a prom taking place at the hotel. Girls in strapless gowns, lifting their skirts, straightening their nylons, fluffing their hair, fixing their makeup, chattering — and staring at me, in my black jacket and dress pants. I fled to my table of queers.

The next night, after a day on the floor of ABA wallowing in variant books and people, the owners of lesbian and gay Century Book Club feted us at PS restaurant on Polk Street in San Francisco. Manny is tall and quiet, his partner Mark moustached and lively. I found them both highly principled, committed to positive images and optimism in gay literature. Over and over as they talked it was obvious they are, rather than a threat to gay and women's bookstores, a lifeline of gay culture. They serve more women customers than men, a fact I didn't expect since men traditionally have more money than women. But men also have greater access to gay books. Mark tells of the letter of thanks they received from a woman who lives on 73rd Street in NYC, near Womanbooks. She cannot afford, she wrote, to be seen going into a women's bookstore, much less buying lesbian books. It's *this* market and those women and men living far from our bookstores that CBC reaches. Commonly they received checks printed Mr. and Mrs. at the top. It is Mrs. who has ordered the books.

My heart filled with hope at this story, as it did each time I looked down Gay Press Row and saw our literature, solid and undeniable, our culture wending its way into places where queers can buy it, absorb it, grow stronger for seeing our lives in print. Next year, who knows, perhaps some of those married ladies will be writing their own books, starting their own presses. Certainly, they may be finding the courage to walk into women's bookstores.

I'm closing in the air, somewhere over South Dakota, full of the excitement of thirty-six hours living and breathing gay publishing. I read this morning that the city of New York is going to paint a lavender line along the Christopher Street Parade route. It's hard to keep myself from peering out the window, searching the midwestern plains for just such a marking — from Gay Press Row back in San Francisco, all the way to New York City — along the Amazon Trail.

Feast Without Fear

I had the honor of sharing the thirteenth anniversary of Portland, Oregon's A Woman's Place Bookstore. The store's three rooms were stuffed with books, periodicals, records and cards. Its staff bustled, its customers perused and picked and paid. It was just-spring and there, on an otherwise nondescript street corner, thrived one of the relatively new species of flora to decorate the Amazon Trail: feminist and gay bookstores.

The celebration took me back to the beginning of those bookstores. I'd heard of them early on, but couldn't imagine — what would they be like? Would the women's bookstores be overgrown libraries of dull political tracts, George Sand and the Brontes where radical collectives would discuss to death the political implications of each purchase? Would the gay stores be hives of the newly liberated thumbing through ancient editions of Renault's *Middle Mist* and Corey's *The Homosexual In America?*

To be honest, I was afraid to investigate. Buying lesbian books had always been such a look-over-my-shoulder ordeal that I couldn't shake the habit. Now I'd be marked, not by going to a certain shelf, nor by taking to the counter one of *those* books — usually upside down or backwards or with a thumb over the title — *now* I had to worry about entering a whole damn store!

At first I'd slip anonymously over the Connecticut border into New York City, grateful I wouldn't have to return through customs. The Oscar Wilde Bookstore originally stood just off Eighth Street in Greenwich Village and I skulked past the lingering sixties phenomena of love bead stores, hookah stores, poster stores and stoned panhandlers, feeling more daring than I ever had patronizing a gay bar. Books, words, these were somehow more legitimate, certainly more powerful, than the liquid wares offered at the bars. And I, seeking them where I did, must certainly be guilty of something — perhaps theft? Did women, gays, really have the right to our own words? Judy Grahn's brilliant title suggests what is behind our specialized purveyors of power: *Gay Words, Gay Worlds.* One leads to the other.

The Oscar Wilde may well have been the first blossom in our springtime. That location was tiny, but was all the space needed as we had so few books to offer each other! To me, it was a space as sacrosanct as any on earth. If I hadn't been so nervous, so self-conscious, and the store so crowded (it had to serve, after all, one tenth of the earth's English-speaking population and had no competition) I might have stood swaying before the shelves, just beaming and breathing the scent of all that purple paper.

I was too frightened to stay long. Surely the salespeople must be made of better stuff than I, be ordained in a way I could never be. I didn't care to stay in their way. And I didn't have to. I clutched my precious prize: the original small press edition of Isabel Miller's *A Place For Us,* later to be reprinted in hardcover as *Patience and Sarah.* Oh, to be a lesbian writer, to inspire others as Miller did me, to be one of the pioneers!

Once I'd managed the gay bookstore hurdle, and even learned to be somewhat comfortable there, I was ready to enter a women's bookstore. Djunabooks, also in the Village, was my next adventure. I found it even more intimidating. Customers had to ring a bell and be buzzed in, a system popular then with the city's jewelers, but here it was used to keep men out! At the time I thought it a great liberating idea — once I got inside.

In time, I didn't even have to travel to New York. Bloodroot opened in Bridgeport, Connecticut, Womonfyre ironically near Emily Dickinson's Mt. Holyoke, and others all over. For a long time the shelves remained to me like someone's precious personal library. Did I dare touch the books? At the lesbian sections, which swelled year after year, I wanted one of each, and went broke indulging my perverted tastes.

Because I was *still* hungry — maybe always would be hungry, for books about me. About the gay life. About women.

Years before anyone had ever dreamed of Rubyfruit Books in Tallahassee, Florida, Womanbooks in New York, Old Wives Tales in San Francisco, Giovanni's Room, Fan the Flames, Women and Children First, Full Circle, Mother Kali's, Golden Thread and on and on, that hunger led me to my first gay lit on a paperback rack in a card shop. I'd just come out, fifteen years old and lost, really lost. The book was *The Well of Loneliness*. Great. But I devoured it despite the scars it would leave on my newly forming psyche and was grateful for the distorted mirror Radclyffe Hall, truly a pioneer, provided me. Instead of satisfying it, *The Well* fed my hunger, and led me on to buy *The Ladder*, Ann Bannon, Valerie Taylor, Vin Packer, Ann Aldrich. Tragic, most of these books, and undermining, but they were all we had.

Until the bookstores and their intimate relations, women's and gay publishers and presses. Like hardy grasses pushing up through the cracked sidewalks of cities everywhere, those cultural oases just get tougher. Gay's the Word of London and Lambda Passages of Miami have endured raids and confiscations of the books that merely depict our lives. Women's bookstores, some bravely facing towns full of threatening bigots, harassing civil servants and physical damage, refuse to close down. I know now that I was right — these bookstore people *are* made of special stuff. I celebrate all of them: the undercapitalized owners, the generous volunteers, the persistent customers — for creating and sustaining these citadels of our culture, these guarantors of our future.

Whether it's Sarah Koehl at A Woman's Place in Oregon, or the Bloodroot Collective in Connecticut, the bookstore staffs tend something very much like a garden, and their crop accomplishes something very much like feeding the hungry. Nowadays, I can feast without fear.

The Fire Within

Forest fires so large, so hungry, so devastating they
are named. Deadwood Summit Fire, Burnt Peak, Angel,
Savage Creek, Cowboy. Firefighters, many of them
women, some of them dykes from the local community,
trying to "control," to "contain," to "line," the blazes.
"Hot spots" flaring up. Flames "jumping" lines, creeks,
the freeway. Two weeks of this havoc, so far, in Southern
Oregon, and the air finally clear enough to see the ring of
mountains around our little valley. My headaches are

receding, smoke-induced irritability is disappearing. Crazed thinking and behavior lessening as the fumes of burning marijuana patches hidden deep in remote woods thin, blow away.

Eleven days into this natural siege, Girlfriend and I both dared to leave home with no one on watch. We drove south for an hour and a quarter, never once leaving the smoke, to see a performance of *The Member of the Wedding*. I'd read Carson McCullers' original novel in early adolescence, when the fires in me had been raging. Now the work's meaning for me as a lesbian rekindles and smolders toward memory and comprehension of how it is to grow up gay in this society.

I saw the start of the fire known as the Longwood Complex which eventually consumed 9916 acres. Girlfriend and I were traveling back from an afternoon jaunt at a California beach. We were ten miles south of the Oregon border. Across the sky flashed violent, stark, merciless jagged white electrical lines. We hoped aloud that the lightning storm would pass quickly and without event. Then we crested a hill and saw, to the east, in a split second, a tall green conifer become a column of red and yellow and orange brilliance. This quick and brutal autumn frightened us. We stopped at the bug station (California still guards its borders against Medflies and their ilk). The inspector was already out on the road, watching the tinder-dry forest burst, tree by tree, into flame. Yes, she knew, she told us with waves and nods when we stopped.

And we stopped again, in O'Brien, Oregon, at a honky-tonk restaurant called Twin Pines Cafe (said with a twang). The place had been remodeled since my last visit. Now it looked like a down-home Denny's. Watching the people during our quick dinner, though, we saw that

51

they were still all country. We left them: waitresses, cook, the owner, standing in the purple night outside the cafe, lighted by their neon, staring up at the mountain now crowned with plumes of smoke. "That's Takilma!" one said. "I live just past the Takilma Store," said another. We sped home through the lukewarm summer night. Lightning escorted us all the way.

I remember how odd I felt in that cafe. If there were not the distraction of the fire, would they have noticed my dykey clothes, watched me walk in my dykey way? I felt as out of place as Frankie Addams did in *The Member of the Wedding.*

"I have never been so puzzled."

"But puzzled about what?"

"The whole thing," Frankie said.

No matter what she did, Frankie could not belong. I identified with her totally: a tomboy, a creative little girl with leadership characteristics which were squelched, a child who was, well, *queer.* Frankie, macho, pried splinters from her callused feet with a carving knife. Frankie, lonely, deviate, who played with littler kids to escape the rites of puberty, yet felt a restless burning inside to clearly belong somewhere, to enter a world which simply seemed not to exist. Now we know, from McCuller's biography, that the author was gay. Frankie's burning was inside McCullers, too.

The fires drove people out of where they belonged, threatened their belongings, their belonging. Evacuations began the second day of burning, and rose to well over 3000 people before the first week was out. One fire near us was left unattended, to burn at will. The area was without roads and there were no structures close enough to cause concern. They said. We were (still are) surrounded on three sides by fire. I filled a box with

52

unfinished manuscripts and stacked the cat carriers outside, ready to go. We had head-counts, the cats and I, twice daily. Like everyone else in the area, Girlfriend and I resigned ourselves to loss, took stock of what we could live without. The important thing was to escape alive if it came to that.

It came to that for Frankie Addams, as it comes to that for every gay child. Attracted by palpable love, Frankie fell in love, said black housekeeper Bernice, with "the weddin'." Frankie's brother and his new wife were obviously happy. They would leave town and travel to far-off places. Odd-girl-out Frankie, who knew nothing but how hard she wanted *something,* fell in love with the romance of them. McCullers made clear that Frankie had no idea what a marriage entailed. What sex was. The girl wanted the feeling exuded by this couple. They belonged to each other and, by the act of marriage, to the world. Frankie knew no other way of coming to belong. She flung herself after them, pleaded to be a part of them. Her exclusion was beyond her comprehension.

I felt bewildered like Frankie at nature's cruelty as more and more acreage was burned. I pondered explanations, for reasons behind these apparently senseless conflagrations. Was nature declaring war on humans, beating back our slow, insidious encroachment, self-immolating before the loggers could steal more of her growth? I agree completely that we had no place in her deepest lairs, that humankind is destructive, mindless, uncaring of her delicate secrets.

But all the little animals? Where would they go? How could they escape? Why force this awful end on them? It's like sending little children into the world gay — and defenseless against the hatred and denial we find.

Bit by bit I got my answers. For three years running we've had drought conditions in this area. The living creatures, from rattlesnakes to deer, have been feeding ever closer to settlements because they've been running out of food. A forest fire, by felling what it does, creates new growth. There will be grazing green on the mountainsides like these animals have not seen in years. Their numbers will increase and they will flourish — until the next cycle begins. Local officials reported that *no* animal carcasses had been found in the fires' wake. Nature takes care of her own.

By the end of *The Member of the Wedding* Frankie tries another way to belong. She pushes and squeezes herself into the box she believes she must fit. To prove that she possesses heterosexual inclinations, she makes much of a schleppy little boy from the neighborhood named Barney. She's wearing a dress instead of a B.V.D. undervest. She's got a girl friend. One watches this frail stick of a human child. She's tense with the effort of convincing herself and proving to others that she belongs by making inappropriate speeches. The audience laughs. I don't think McCullers meant this as comedy. I cry for my own perplexed little girl, thirty years ago, who postured like Frankie, trying on the straight world. But oh, Frankie, your telltale dreams! She and her new girlfriend will travel to Europe, she says, will journey to romantic places together, just like the married couple.

Gay children flare up everywhere, stronger than religion and law and violence. Frankie Addams was probably my first variant role model, a message from sexually confused McCullers that I was not the only one. I had no name for the society to which Frankie wanted to belong, but I saw her approach it, want it just like me, saw

54

it hidden by the straight adults, saw it elude her. Her yearning, though, assured me it was there. And I found it. Nature takes care of her own.

My Summer Vacation

I've been exhausted for ten years. That's how long it's been since I started writing fiction steadily, without a break. Even in the year that I was ill for six months, moved cross country, ended a thirteen-year relationship, began a new one and two new jobs, I wrote sporadically, whenever I felt I would go nuts if I didn't. Some call it workaholism. I called it necessity.

Still, one gets tired. I decided to take this month off. I'm still doing columns and book reviews and research for the new book and, of course, my job, but my pace has slowed to a state I can experience as vacation.

During this break I've been able to muse about the source of my exhaustion. How did it all start, this merry-go-round of writing, touring, working all the harder for a living to make up for the time I take out to write? I know it was about September of 1979 that I enrolled in a Yoga class and stopped eating meat. I was trying to change my life in a positive way. That November I saw a chiropractor for tendonitis. He told me to stop doing alcohol, caffeine and processed foods. After all, I'd stopped smoking — I could handle the rest. By about February of 1980 I'd even eased off a twenty-three year tranquilizer diet.

But I need to go back even further than that, to the change that made room in my life for all this health consciousness. I have to go back to *Rocky*.

Now, I know this will sound strange. I know it's totally inappropriate for a lesbian writer to have found inspiration for her renewed career at the movies, especially *that* movie, but there are extenuating circumstances. This was before my life-changing trip to the chiropractor who is the same man who discovered my allergy to corn. One of the effects corn has on my system is to heighten my emotions. You know, at a sad movie, I get hysterical and cry my heart out; at a comic movie I become euphoric. Why at the movies? Pop*corn*. I'm an American. I loved to consume popcorn at the movies. Plus, there's some direct relationship between allergy and addiction which I don't quite understand. It's likely that I not only ate this poison in theaters, but that I indulged in an intemperate manner.

So there I was watching *Rocky*. Corn fumes wafted like invisible San Francisco fog around me. I fed myself more. Sylvester Stallone was on the screen, bigger than life, an underdog just like me — well, maybe not *just* like me — but he was a boxer who hadn't made it, I was a writer in the same situation. Then, through sheer gumption and courage, Rocky transforms himself into a winner. He stood atop those famous steps, jumping up and down like a fool, and I, whipped even further into a vulnerable high by this visual challenge and the feverishly inspirational music, identified completely with him. If Rocky Balboa could do it, then so could this little dyke whose mission was certainly more important than Rocky's. I flexed my literary biceps, my linguistic pectorals. *I* would do for other lesbians what Jane Rule and Isabelle Miller had done for me: given me hope and a view of the lesbian would through glasses untainted by doom. I would give writing one more try.

By October of 1977 I had switched from a job which required my presence at least ten hours each day, to one where I worked thirty-five hours a week. I began then, with Rocky-like courage, to train my imagination, build my writing skills, and most of all to build up discipline until I used every available minute for my writing. I bussed to work so I could plot stories as I commuted. I found ways to get my job done in fewer hours so that I could write lesbian fiction at my desk. I *scheduled* time with friends and with my lover. Sick days at work I hoarded to whip out stories. Sleep I cut back so badly that I developed insomnia. When I did go to bed, I'd put myself to sleep dreaming up characters, only to wake myself and write them down. Not a moment or an ounce of energy was wasted. It all, worthy or not, went into lesbian literature.

What drove me? I was frightened, almost literally to death, of not finishing what I wanted, needed to, before my clock ran out and death, or homophobia, stopped me for good.

At first, I didn't understand that I was wearing myself out. I was so very happy to be writing again, believed so avidly in my cause, that it was a new intoxication: I felt no pain. As the years wore on, though, I had no energy for normal human endeavors like housecleaning or relationships. I called myself lazy, felt fatigued, blamed it on growing old, on gruesome diseases, learned to meditate. Nothing seemed to help. My health broke down, finally, from the overwork and other causes, but when I recovered, I was right back in that ring slugging it out with time and energy.

Then, a couple of months ago, I went to the dentist. He told me about a lecture given by a former NASA physician who'd been on the scene when death felled a series of NASA engineers. Foul play was suspected, but research revealed overwork to be the villain. These professionals, whether from competitiveness, passion or workaholism, ran on adrenalin highs. All joggers, they kept that jogging high in everything they did, pacing themselves, as it turned out, beyond human endurance.

This disturbed me, but then came the clincher. Girlfriend, whom most of you know as Tee Corinne, artist, art critic, lecturer, had been finishing a book of erotic prose and poetry called *Dreams of the Woman Who Loved Sex* (Banned Books.) Suddenly, I was the one living with a writer — the tables, or tablets, were turned. The day I realized I'd been watching Tee act out my behavior patterns I just laughed. How in the world could she *stand* to live with me when I'm working? I mean, artists have their crazies, too, but the transformation of a human being into a writer is just plain scary.

We act stubborn, are not terribly sensible, let our priorities get all topsy-turvy, obsess to the point of living out characters' lives, drive ourselves beyond exhaustion and go half-crazed with the effort of balancing an impossible number of thematic, plot and character threads in our teeny human brains. And always, that terror of not having enough time, that race against silence before the words are all said.

No wonder I — and Girlfriend — are exhausted. I'm hoping this break will teach me something about balancing myself. Though I'm scared I'll never be able to pick up the thread of writing again afterward, that my discipline will collapse, that I'll be unable to function without the adrenalin engine revving, that I'll run out of time — I'm more scared of running out of life. What tragic irony, should any of us die trying to outrun death, or its equivalent for the gay writer, the grim censor.

The Isles of Lesbos

Jane Rule, like Sappho, lives on an island. Is this coincidence, or a signpost to success for all of us singers of lesbian tales? Is the island the perfect lesbian literary zone? A realm of seclusion, inspiration and safety?

Djuna Barnes wrote *Nightwood* in Peggy Guggenheim's castle, another sort of island. Janet Flanner wrote her New Yorker column from the top floor of a Paris hotel. Katherine Hulme, author of *The Nun's Story,* lived with her lover in that same hotel. I visited the late lesbian writer, Elsa Gidlow, where she wrote on a California mountaintop.

Recently, I happened to speak with a literary agent in New York City. When I mentioned my little domicile, she exclaimed, "You live in a *trailer*!??" Already awed by her function in the world, I stammered out some feeble excuse for such a non-traditional dwelling. Yet I love it. And I'm not the only one. Texas writer Tony Azolakov (*Cass and the Stone Butch*) is another trailer-dweller. Surely our tin castles are the equivalent at least of the poet's garret, the artist's loft?

I don't need an island, a castle. I'm remembering Willa Cather in her brownstone on Washington Square in New York City's Greenwich Village. She had the City teeming around her, she was on the doorstep of world culture, a bohemian paradise filled the view from her windows. Ah! What a place to write, to think, to dream! Yet she's the one who tells us that the source of all our inspiration comes not from these exciting and distracting stimuli, but from the first few years of our lives.

It is amazing the worlds we fit inside our minds. And amazing that this diminutive home of mine can hold them all. Eight feet wide and, bumper to bumper, thirty-one feet long, I'm squeezed inside with New York City, New England, Chicago, San Francisco and all my other story sites. Yet there's room for the four cats and Girlfriend's dog and cat, for Girlfriend herself.

Margaret Anderson edited *The Little Review* one summer in a tent beside Lake Michigan. Carson McCullers had to leave her regular life and move periodically into writers' colonies to weave her lovingly grotesque yarns. From my chair in the front of my two rooms, I can see crisscrossing black tree trunks and branches, leaves and graceful featherings of evergreen needles swaying in the breezes against a backdrop of darkening valley sky. Thomas, my gay male cat whose lover died this time of year two summers ago, comes through the cat door with a "breep," looking appalled at the sight of me occupying His (the only) comfortable chair. He moves to his food and I listen to him sing while he eats. I am content.

Monique Wittig wrote for a time on the rocky coast of California; May Sarton, on the craggy coast of Maine. I can sit on my porch to write or just gaze at the bird population, the deer, the occasional skunk or porcupine, the cows in the pasture next door. I built the porch for Sweetpea, my disabled cat. She couldn't make it down the steps to the kitty bathroom, so I brought it up to her. It only seemed logical to extend the porch for human use and it now houses my former living room furniture, has a roof to protect me from the sometimes brutal sun, and "bamboo" shades to give Girlfriend and me some privacy during daring outdoor cuddles.

Natalie Barney lived on the Rue Jacob in Paris; Marilyn Hacker in a tiny Parisian studio at the end of a flight of countless ancient stairs. Did Barney hang Romaine Brooks' work floor to ceiling in her home? I have little wall space, but Tee Corinne covers the bulk of it. Post card art, of course, is the logical trailer decoration. I've managed a Utrillo flush against the floor under a front room window, a bulletin board of photographs on the wall into which my mini-refrigerator is set. A collage hangs over the plastic toilet, maps line my hallway of closets.

I love the uniqueness of trailer space. The necessity for creative solutions. The efficiency demanded by living in miniature. I'm seated, though, next to built-in shelving in which I've stored cannisters. They are round, with rounded tops. Into the gaps between them I've stuck my grandfather's harmonica which I've been dragging around for twenty years and never learned to play, a folded yardstick I can never find, a stack of canned veggies hoarded for the winter when snow will stop the pass or the bomb will finally fall. Terrible use of space! I need to put in another shelf, or to buy a new set of flat, close-fitting, efficient canisters at Goodwill.

These challenges make living in a trailer like writing short stories. A novel is roomy, with castle-like spaces, mountaintops from which to view the world, whole islands upon which to set characters roaming. In a short story, Sally the Bartender, Henny the fruit-seller, sober Jefferson must pace a limited world. Every thought and word must count and help to shape the whole. My mind functions best in literature's travel trailers, in housing's short stories. I love having the options to fold my dinner table into the wall, to slide my bedroom door away like some character in a story who only appears in order to move the plot along.

Ann Bannon wrote the Beebo Brinker series while married in suburbia. Valerie Taylor completed *Prism* in a second-floor apartment in otherwise unromantic Margaretville, N.Y. Emily Dickinson wrote her poetry and mooned over her sister-in-law from her bedroom. Presumably there are women everywhere writing their way out of marriage, writing about their lives, writing the love they can express in no other way. Writing on islands of their own making, in the castles of their minds.

Me, I've got this '72 Holiday Rambler named Josephine. She's what's called in the industry "self-contained," a term meant to refer to her plumbing. But self-contained she is, the stomping ground of this dyke's imagination. My rural garret is yet another

solution to the poor writers' syndrome, another place a
lesbian can seek inspiration, solitude, safety: a Western
island in drydock.

GAY RITES

Dykes in the Western Bible Belt

You don't realize how deep your roots go till you pull them up. How where you've been, who you've been there with and what you did have shaped, or bent, or straightened you. Though I never feel straightened, in Oregon, I sometimes feel bent.

Girlfriend, who's Floridian by birth, and therefore familiar with phenomena like a lot of sky, or which wind is likely to be a harbinger of rain, or sunsets, was discussing the location of something or other on her rural land. She said it was west of where we stood.

"You mean near the stream?"

"Creek. In Oregon it's a creek. And no, I mean west," she said with certainty.

I looked around me, envisioned a compass in my head, but just like in Girl Scouts, didn't know which way to point it so I'd know where the rest of it went.

Kindly, patiently, she said, "The sun. Think where the sun rises, where it sets."

Once more I scrinched up my eyes and envisioned like crazy. I just couldn't visualize it. I had no idea where the sun rose or set.

Girlfriend groaned, but not for the reasons I would have preferred. "Think," she instructed me, for luckily she'd also lived in New York City where I was raised, "of the house up the road as the Bronx and the creek as the Hudson River."

"Oh!" I said happily. "The Bronx is north. So the stream *is* west. The creek," I corrected myself quickly.

See what I mean? I've carried the city with me so thoroughly I think in city language.

So it is, too, with living on the Amazon Trail. We carry our culture with us wherever we go.

My friend Sue the Intrepid Hitchhiker, for example, called this week. In her progress from Portland to my home, she managed to weave herself in and out of a net of ever more southerly dykes who welcomed her presence, her stories; fed her, gave her beds and rides and generally helped avoid all but the briefest encounters with anyone of the het persuasion.

Once here she butted in and out of my workroom as I readied material for *On Our Backs,* a magazine of lesbian erotica.

70

Once more, Sue had horned into a lesbian nest.

And Christmas. What do dykes do in the Western Bible Belt to survive Christmas? Why travel the Amazon Trail to celebrate it, of course.

We had a party on the day of Winter Solstice. Complete with a Christmas tree and huge turkey devoured by meat eaters and vegetarians alike. From as far north as Eugene came an assortment of dykes whose lesbianism colors their perspectives as clearly as my city-bias colors the country.

There were Daphne and Judith whose store "It's a Natural" on 2nd Avenue, in Myrtle Creek has become a lesbian and gay connection along the Amazon Trail. Then there was Charlotte Mills of Bookmakers in Eugene, a teacher of self-publishing whose expertise is inspiring a host of lesbians to preserve and disperse our culture on paper. An improvisational actress whose personal theater group entertains dykes as well as depicting us, was there. A woman who teaches bookbinding, another who earns her living making false teeth and is turning that skill into art, another who's an avid reader and therefore supporter of lesbian authors and presses, a doctoral candidate who'll soon be another lesbian teaching women's herstory — they were all there along with the little boy lucky enough to be growing up in the midst of us.

They all took turns reading from my self-published story "Christmas At a Bar," a lesbian Christmas story. As Girlfriend said by way of introduction to the story: "We need both to create new celebrations and to claim and reclaim old ones."

And we did just that. We followed, finally, paper bag lanterns to a bonfire and sat singing a mix of spirituals and dyke songs into the cold dark night. We celebrated our varied cultures: religious, women's, lesbian, with our

71

varied voices blending — or not blending — but all creating a voice in the night, a strong clear one brought together by the invisible thread of the Amazon Trail.

I sang too. Furtively nostalgic. After all, weren't we gathered just south of the Bronx, listening to the flow of the Hudson River?

Tale of a Tourist

One of my cats died last night, after I'd returned from a glorious day at Crater Lake. My old friend Carol Lynne, briefly here from Connecticut, was with me for both the death and the trip.

Edison, the cat, was thirteen. He'd lost his mother at an early age and been adopted by a dyke who moved in with my ex-lover and me in Connecticut. When the dyke took off for Florida, Edison became ours, and when I broke with the lover, Edison became mine. He was overweight and overbearing, arrested somewhere around infancy where food and affection were concerned, craving abnormal amounts of both. But he was a handsome cat, formal in his constant tuxedo, and loving. The official greeter in my household, I couldn't keep him off a guest's lap, wanted or not.

But he'd had cystitis for years. An operation helped temporarily, medication helped to a point, tomato juice, with its crystal-dissolving powers, kept him going a while longer. I buried him this morning, under a crooked tree, the first occupant of a pet cemetery Girlfriend and I envision. We're planning an Edison Memorial Seat under the crooked tree. She baked an Edison Memorial Cake. And I'm left trying to make sense of the impermanence of life. How we seem to just pass through it, like tourists in a park. Why just yesterday, I'd think, tears welling up, Eddy was running after mice in the back field. Or last time I looked, there he was, sleeping in his regal black and white robes on my bed.

Then there's Carol, my old friend. Last night she was still here too, and we sat sharing the nearly wordless signals of twenty years of friendship. We met in college, she a freshman, I a sophomore, both from New York City. We later became lovers, then broke up, joined living collectives, settled separately in New Haven, met often for Chinese dinners and prolonged giggling fits. Keeping our connection gave us both a feeling of continuity, of permanence.

Carol talked about another college friend, from whom she seems to have grown away. About how relationships, friends, change. About how people, pets, pass through, sometimes out of our lives, and we through theirs. She comforted me with talk of Gordie, her diabetic cat, who finally died after years of insulin shots and four "Last

Birthday" parties. At each of these celebrations she'd ply him with lox and smoked whitefish. I was there for each party. This year, I would not have been, but we celebrated Carol's birthday the night before Edison's death. Funny little rituals of lesbian life. The ways we make family, to keep, and let go of, one another.

So yesterday, one specific yesterday in twenty years of them, Carol and I toured Crater Lake Park, talking of Gordie, old friends, college, New York, our new lives and lovers, of how it is to be queer in the world, of how queer it is to be in the world.

The park was riotous with bold life. Even before we reached it we stopped to behold a gorge, its water, in otherwise dry Southern Oregon, bursting along a path through the rocks, hurrying, shouting, as sure as *we'd* been twenty years before. We tried to capture that quick life with cameras.

We drove through a forest of mammoth pines teeming with every living thing indigenous to these parts. We rounded the rim of Crater Lake to behold that first breathtaking wondrous view. The lake, so many thousand feet below, was a piercing blue, mellowed by lush green coves. Boatloads of people were like toys in a bathtub. Large birds wheeled above, defying the frightening heights. We, too, climbed as far as we could and timorously peered over edges. Mosses, flowers, pines, madrones, insects, more birds. Nothing, despite the holy silence, was still. We were tiny transient lives amongst many, clinging, like the hardy white pines, to our own rocky promontories. Building, like the birds, nest after nest. Nourishing ourselves, like the deer, on the greenery of our lives: friendships, loves — hearty foods both. Tiny chipmunks darted up and down the cliffs. The cliffs, the mountains, longer lasting, more significant than a thousand chipmunks, trees, Carol, me, Edison.

Then Edison who'd died, all warm and soft and furry, in my arms. I walked around today stunned, weeping, knowing full well his death had to come. But after a day like that? In the face of all that life? After Crater Lake, after his morning exploits with the mice?

As if to emphasize the passing of all things, Carol left today, to return to her/my old life back east.

I called a new friend. She's eighty and wise with common sense. "How," I asked her, "can I reconcile these things? Life and loss? Death and unstoppable, boisterous being?"

"You know," she said, not even pausing to think, "Crater Lake is the result of a kind of death. It was created by a volcano that caused incredible destruction. And we're left with a beautiful, beautiful lake we wouldn't have had without that death."

We all pass through our Crater Lakes.

Love Rites

How many of us have wished, at one time or another, for a means to formalize our loves, to publicly celebrate our bondings? Straight people may have something in their marriage rituals, may be adding a cement that strengthens the tie through a public demonstration of respect for the relationship and the lovers involved. On the other hand a ceremony may well, as its detractors argue, put demands on a relationship that weakens it. But for those gays who long to walk down an aisle . . .

Recently, Girlfriend and I were invited to such a bonding here in Southern Oregon. It was a lesson to me in community as family. And in the community's power to affirm, to turn well-wishing into visible energy. I'm sharing it here for those who've never witnessed such a ceremony, for those designing their own, and for all you sentimentalists who just love a wedding.

Rose, mother of one of the brides, had called us, pleased and proud. We were thrilled to be able to participate in this rural lesbian ceremony and on the big night donned the most traditionally wedding-like apparel we could invent. Girlfriend wore her diaphanous, bright blue flowered caftan and pants combination. I, my thrift store chinos and black velour jacket, a new boys' size white shirt and a black tie with the word *dyke* blazoned across it.

The wedding was held in Elea's older farm house. She works a multi-acred ranch with Rose's help.

Now, Rose and Elea are a story in themselves. Rose has shown us a photograph of herself as a teenager. If I'd met her on a Greenwich Village street back then, I might have thought she was Beebo Brinker fresh from the farm. Except neither Beebo nor I had been born yet. Rose is at retirement age. She also was married. Because that's what one did back then more often than not. Over the years she had a son, a bright star in her life who was a talented writer and died in Vietnam. Fortunately, she also had Edna, a girl who seemed troubled, was more difficult, apparently, to communicate with.

Elea, who is Roses' age, married too, and the couples became friends. Moved out to Oregon at the same time. Rose and Elea owned a business and eventually became interested in metaphysical religion. They would do past life regressions together and kept discovering that they'd been close in other lives. Sometimes as a married couple. After a while it became clear to them that in this life too, theirs was the real marriage, not their conventional ones. They separated from their husbands and became lovers after thirty years of friendship.

So the wedding, in effect, took place at the parental home. And by this time, obviously, Rose and her daughter Edna weren't having as much trouble communicating. Edna had grown into a tall, strong-looking telephone line repairperson vaguely resembling that early picture of her mother. When her mother came out to her, Edna, of course, admitted she'd been a dyke all along.

Among the guests assembled in the farmhouse were Pearl, author and Ph.D. at a nearby college. She wore a royal blue velvet gown with an elegantly embroidered bodice. Scottie, a retired computer repairperson, wore jeans and a crisp flannel shirt, her short white hair neatly combed into a butchy little wave. She'd arrived with Betty, the straight sister of a man active in the local gay organization.

Zintara, a tall, broad-shouldered, laughing young woman, wore a white Indian-style shirt and lavender scarf with grey cords and velcro-closure sneakers. With her was J.P., also dressed to the nines in red tie, pink shirt and jeans.

Jim, the official photographer who'd decorated the house opulently with forsythia, daffodils and wild plum blossoms, talked about his life. Because he's gay, he'd lost jobs with the Forest Service (would he fondle young trees? Give secrets to Soviet bird-spies?) and then as the clinical psychologist of the local school system. Now he's exploring his spirituality, listening to his female side. He may not have any better vocational luck, but he finds great inspiration in feminist theology, which he sees as neither matriarchal nor patriarchal, but a blending of the best of female and male thought.

Edna and her lover Sharon, a Californian, were to be joined in a Metropolitan Community Church ceremony by Glenn Scott. Blonde, of medium height, with a stillness about him, Glenn had recently resigned as pastor of the local MCC chapter and was on his way to L.A. to become a student at Samaritan College. He hoped to go out to new communities later to build congregations. In his cream-colored cords, short-sleeved white shirt with reversed collar, he explained the rite he was about to perform.

"The Rite of Blessing," Glenn said in his soft, clear voice, "avoids the role model relationships in a traditional marriage. It's a model that works for gay people, encouraging us to make commitments to openness and honesty in our relationships. Its purpose is to affirm the relationship rather than lead people to make a lot of promises they can't keep."

He looked away to smile at those busily readying the living room for its new role. "Usually, the couple takes six months after a Rite of Blessing to explore the relationship. Then we perform a 'Holy Union' ceremony which is MCC's closest counterpart to holy matrimony."

The musicians signalled that they were ready. The guitarist wore a red shirt, black vest, black pants and black cowboy boots. Her lover Marty, in a checkered gingham dress, is deacon at the MCC. Both are also active in a fundamentalist Christian church where they are not out. Marty's daughter, in blue plaid western shirt and bandana neckerchief, was the singer. She cuts wood to earn a living, but also has her own, male, country western band. *Her* young daughter bustled about with a purple flower adorning her hair. "Are they ready?"

stage-whispered someone and we all took seats in the living room.

While the musicians began "Could I Have This Dance For the Rest of My Life?" the brides entered, stately, with an excited radiance emanating from their nervous faces. Edna was resplendent in a brown, wide-lapeled western-style suit edged in white piping. Her ruffled shirt protruded at the cuffs with light-catching gold cufflinks. She wore a brown western-style bow tie. Her lover Sharon was shorter, soft-looking, and her dark eyes sparkled over a herring-bone wool jacket and black slacks, a white shirt and short black tie. Rose stood beside Edna in a simple red velour top, grey slacks and white necklace, while Elea stood next to Sharon in a purple velour top over dark slacks.

Glenn was on the other side of a long table decorated with a white cloth and flowers. There were more flowers behind him on his mantle. With a shy grin on his face he began to tell the story of this wedding day. Long before dawn that morning Elea had called them all to help pull a calf. Glenn had never been part of a calving before, but there he was, with the brides, the mother of the bride, Elea and Jim, up to their knees in mud, two pushing, two pulling "in order for that life to come forth." The cow and its calf would both have died, he said, just as a relationship can die without a life support system such as the one he'd been part of that morning. He likened the MCC rituals to that life support system. He urged Sharon and Edna to find their "best wholeness" and the rest of us to "send them energy."

The couple read a statement they had written in which they pledged to meet one another's needs, to love and not condemn one another.

"I love you," said Edna.

"I love you," answered Sharon. There were wet eyes around the room as they exchanged rings and the singer began "Let the Rest of the World Go By."

Glenn blessed the relationship; Rose turned to sprinkle rose petals over Edna and Sharon, saying "I'm *proud* of you!" Elea then sprinkled her petals over them and all reached out to touch one another and Glenn while they prayed quietly.

Glenn sang then, closing the ceremony. The room became solemnly still until Rose laughed, reaching to hug her new daughter-in-law. In her western accent, Rose said, "I never thought I'd have such a *short* kid!" So the celebration began with laughter.

Bottles popped and Sharon vowed to keep the first bottle of strawberry champagne forever. There, in the small happy crowd, watching the couple open their wedding gifts, were Fundamentalist Christians, a Roman Catholic, Metaphysicians and followers of women's spirituality. Most of us were gay, but some were straight; men and women mixed comfortably. We were united in caring for this young couple's happiness and future. We were celebrating their love as openly as we dared, in ways gay people had to invent.

Pearl, Girlfriend and I drove back in the dark through the monumental Southern Oregon mountains. Spring was beginning to make itself visible in the softness of the hills, in the smell of the air without a hint of frost. Questions went through my mind as fast as the telephone poles went past the car's windows. What had I just witnessed? What did it mean in my life?

If I didn't go through such a ceremony was my relationship with my lover any less? With one, would we stay together any longer? And what about Pearl, liking her single lifestyle? Was there no ceremony of affirmation for her?

Because it *had* felt good, that gathering of friends who brought gifts of love and luck to Sharon and Edna. Would it feel as good should Girlfriend and I receive the blessings of our community? Wouldn't it be fine if our blood families would or could participate? And would we respect our love — love more deeply somehow — if we celebrated and vowed publicly?

But more immediately, what would happen to that night's brides? Would they make it to the Holy Union? It sure looked as if they would. Their happiness was very apparent, their delight in each other a joy to see. Then — is there a happily ever after for gay bondings?

Perhaps this public declaration will work for Edna and Sharon. How wonderful that such a ceremony can be a choice for them now, for all of us.

Good Magic

Last June I devoted a column to the Bonding Ritual
I'd been privileged to attend. Since then I've given a great
deal of thought to the subject of gay marriage. A great
deal. Girlfriend and I have decided to wed.

We've both come to this decision with certainty after
pondering innumerable issues around marriage for
anyone, and especially marriage for lesbians. I'm still
grappling with some of those issues, because they won't
be resolved by the ceremony alone.

I've tried to think through the subject on my own, and tried also to talk with a therapist about it. But she was straight. Accepting, but straight. How could I trust her to help process what I can't see clearly myself? And why, I wondered, couldn't I see clearly? What was getting in my way?

Then I read Daniel Yates Rist's "Sexual Slander," an article primarily about AIDS in the May 13, 1986 *Advocate*. His premise is that gay men are almost passively accepting the blame for a disease the world at large has conveniently labeled theirs. All in one it is punishment of gays and vindication of straights. AIDS as a symbol is the new pink triangle, a symbol of self-hatred so internalized the victims self-destruct. It's a fantastic article I could recap for the length of the column. But my interest right now is in the self-hatred, and how that applies to me and my struggle with formalizing my love.

Neither the sexual slander of AIDS, says Rist, nor my struggle, will be resolved until "we stop apologizing — for AIDS, our love, our lives." AIDS is, simply, not a gay disease, and marriage not a straight institution. But we believe we must take on the guilt of the disease, and believe we cannot have such a validating tradition as marriage. Rist says, ". . . even were AIDS *cured* today, our failure to believe in our integrity remains . . ."

And it is that illness, the dis-ease of a weak integrity, which haunts me even as I plan to publicly, passionately and permanently join with my mate. Marriage is for good, clean, upstanding citizens. And I am of the community Rist describes as hardly recovered from our "agonizing years believing lies about ourselves, hideous lies that fed self-hate, that ate away at us until we feared any minute we would be destroyed. . . . *Lies* . . . that we cannot love, that we're unlovable, that we're sexually obsessed, that we're all promiscuous, that our relationships don't last."

As I prepare to make my promise, my doubts are not about my partner. No, she's a major miracle in my life and I couldn't be more sure there. What nags at me is my right to the rite, whether I deserve to partake of the blessings marriage is designed to bestow. Rist again: ". . . our marriages and gay families disgust the law." Churches perpetuate the "vulgar lying images of gays . . ." And I, somewhere inside, believe these lies, accept these insults, devalue myself till I fear I'm giving little of worth to my spouse.

Why bother? Why hassle with these "straight" ways? Some lesbians criticize romantic love and marriage as straying into the enemy camp, adopting their ways, betraying our own. Gays have lived for centuries without the ceremony. Surely a bit of mumbo-jumbo intoned by a person of the cloth can't create a spiritual and social superglue that will insure longevity of commitment, that will guarantee continued interest and fidelity.

That's what I always thought while I was refusing to listen to this silly heart of mine which yearned to set a seal on my love. That's what I always told myself when, at a straight wedding, I watched the good will showered on the couple. Why not *us* up there, dignified, regally garbed, beaming and beamed upon?

I researched marriage, to learn its roots and the cultural roots of my yearning. In the Encyclopedia Britannica, under the entry "Marriage," I learned that the ritual was more about property (goods and human children) than about either love or good will. It wasn't until I happened on the entry "Primitive Marriage" that I began to get the answers I sought.

"A marriage rite as a rule is also a ritual act with symbolic significance, and as such is often conceived to have magical efficacy. . . . as perhaps the most important contract ever entered by the marital partners and as an act that creates a new family, marriage is a crisis. A crisis in human life is surrounded by powerful emotions: forebodings and hopes, fears and joyful anticipations. Innumerable rites exist that are associated with the crisis of marriage. . . . The contract is made binding in that members of the community bear witness to it; it is hallowed in that the mates solemnly and openly declare . . . that they belong to each other."

This is what I wanted. A blessing, a witnessing, a bringing down of good magic to a union I choose in order to obey my internal laws. And this is what I demand: the right to such a ceremony. The universe is full of spiritual bounty; let it shower a portion onto us, a lesbian couple, and not reserve it all for heterosexuals. No wonder we've been barred by every court and every religion from partaking of this sacrament — we might feel legitimate, blessed, accepted by the human race and the goddesses!

My own behavior had been the clue to the disturbance in me. In announcing the event I've choked on the word marriage, or have not shared my plans at all. Would people think a marriage between two women weird, distasteful? Be shocked, disapproving? I've longed to present it as if on a platter, this bit of beauty in my life, but I've feared to stumble as I serve it, feared I'd end up staring, embarrassed, at what had become no more than an ugly mess in someone's lap.

The ceremony is not a necessity. The relationship we're living and building will not dissolve without it. I'm not trying to start, or continue, a trend. But I am seeking a way to give myself permission to take whatever good magic is rightfully ours. It's a tough world we live in. Gay unions are as susceptible as any, or more so, to the dangers out- and inside us.

There is evidence that same sex marriages have taken place as long as there has been marriage. These have been legitimate marriages, performed by the clergy of the time in front of everyone. I want to take back just one more thing that's been taken away. But after a lifetime of learning to apologize, learning to believe the lies, learning to feel and accept the legislated disgust, it's hard to feel worthy, hard to take what I want so badly, hard to acknowledge that I *deserve*. It's hard, hard, hard to step away from the world that would deny me the joy and support of a solid healthy love — and to walk up an aisle, and simply take it.

Lesbian Stew

At dinner the other night, a friend suggested that lesbians have a unique relationship with food. What I took to be the essence of her thoughts was this pithy observation: We fuss over food. It is another of the innumerable issues that make us so loveable.

There probably is not a lesbian in the world who would not, at the slightest sign of interest, tell you about her personal history with food. For some, food has been a joy, for others. a struggle. I spent my earliest years swallowing great quantities of evil-tasting stuff called *tonic* in an effort to fatten my skinny frame. One of the most humiliating moments of my childhood was the time my father, rather than take my hand to cross the street, encircled my wrist with his big fingers and laughed at its slightness, like he'd found a pitiable lone toothpick in an otherwise empty jar. We were crossing a busy street in Boston at the time; to this day I can't think of the school, the VFW post, the apartment building on that site without a sense of shame. All those years of nauseating tonics and I still couldn't measure up.

As an adolescent, I wished food could be served powdered, in a capsule, and that the social rituals around it would be banned by the World Health Organization. Dinner Out was the only thing worse than Dinner At Home with the nuclear family. Why in the world groups of people gathered around tables and talked to each other while stuffing their mouths was beyond me. I had what the doctors called a "nervous stomach." They gave me little blue pills, bitter white pills, tiny peach-colored pills. In college, after a little blue pill and some gross imitation of nutrition, I could just barely stagger back to the dorm to pass out. I spent a good part of my first thirty-five years sick to my stomach. Literally. I thought *everyone* went through what I did and, like me, was just too polite to mention it.

Now I know I faced two problems. The first was solved fairly simply: I had food allergies. Some of the most common table foods actually make me ill. The second was much larger and more complex: A need to control my life. It was this latter problem which I suspect is at the bottom of the unique lesbian relationship with food.

Everyone, it is said, is born into this world kicking and squalling. The lesbian child, whatever other strikes she may inherit against her, enters life with two. The female condition has been well documented. But who has talked about butch infants striding around their cribs with clenched fists? Of *femmes fatales* plying their early little charms on every aunt, girl cousin, and housewife-neighbor who peers into their playpens?

I always thought that I came out at fifteen. Last year I delved into a box of family photographs to find images of Little Lee (clothed in a more feminine appellation) dressed in three-piece corduroy pants suits, in flannel-lined dungarees, in overalls. Images of my pre-adolescent self in flannel shirts and jeans, hair slicked back. Or just-adolescent with my sleeves rolled up to my paltry biceps, and unlit parental cigarette hanging from my sneering 11-year-old lips. "Holy shit," I thought, I was gay even back then.

"Holy shit," I say now, no wonder so many of have food issues. If food, as we've learned from research on anorexia and bulimia, is a way of controlling, often the only way of controlling, our young lives, no wonder lesbians wield it like a weapon. Scrawny Little Lee was rejecting everything her innocently straight parents were offering her. "This is the life we want you to live," they told me in a thousand different ways, offering me marriage and my very own family; offering me boys, dresses, homemaker skills; offering me a highly socialized role that my gut knew was dead wrong for me. I rejected their social nourishment — of *course* I'd reject their carrots and spinach and steak. In fact, I suspect my food allergies are no more than a systematic, automatic response my body developed to those foods which most obviously represented to me family life and the golden platter of heterosexuality. I gagged on it.

Enter potlucks, vegetarianism, feminist restaurants, growing our own foods, collective cooking, music festival foodlines.

Enter health foods, allergy testing, rotation diets, organic foods, food coops, *The Political Palates,* and *Red Beans and Rice.*

Enter the concept, shared with other alternative cultures, of taking control of our lives through food. Creating our own rituals around eating. Determining for ourselves what to feed us, how to feed us, with whom we would feed.

Once, after leaving a lover and moving into my own place, Barbara Grier, then editor of *The Ladder,* urged a recipe on me to forestall malnutrition I was likely to have suffered. She told me to cook up some green peppers, onions, rice, hamburger and what all in a great big old frying pan, and then to freeze individual packets of the stuff in foil. Dutifully I took a packet of what I'd dubbed Lesbian Stew from my freezer each day before work and each night when I came home pushed it around the frying pan. I think that was the first time I'd ever fully understood that there was a connection between food and sustaining life — between putting this stew in my mouth and being able to write stories and articles for *The Ladder,* or make love to women, or dance all night.

My cooking repertoire has grown. I've even come to enjoy long solitary nights of baking cookies, the smell of garlic frying in preparation for a rice dish, the way a well-sharpened knife can make paper-thin slices of tomatoes look pretty all soaked in rice vinegar, under a sprinkling of minutely chopped scallions. But more, I've come to almost like digging in with friends, comparing recipes or writing styles or the day's events over a casserole topped with bubbling just-toasted cheese. No longer does anyone serve me promises of motherhood, skills for keeping a husband happy, or Emily Post's recommendations on hostessing.

My body has learned what foods poison it; my queer soul has found tablemates to nourish it; I take great care what I ingest, having been force-fed from an alien menu too long. Where once the little girl stood accused of fretfully fussing over her food, now, lesbian-like, I fuss joyfully over what I know I need, body and soul.

Second-Hand Posh

You meet the most interesting people in thrift stores
— like the time I bumped into my real-estate agent, a
highly made up, very fashionable recent transplant from
L.A. When I'd signed with her, I'd assumed I was dealing
with a successful entrepreneur come to make her fortune
in the untamed promised land, who still flew back to L.A.
to update her wardrobe. Or so I thought until I met her at
the Salvation Army. She didn't want to acknowledge me. I

knew I was in trouble, and I was right. She didn't sell the house.

Nor did I always have a comfortable relationship with second-hand stores. As a kid, just the thought of buying something used embarrassed the heck out of me. Hand-me-downs were bad enough. I came from the kind of family that has two sides: the side that wouldn't shop in a thrift store and doesn't have to; and the side that did, but didn't want to talk about it.

The breakthrough came when I discovered books and the joy of owning them. My compulsive personality found its outlet in collecting when I was too young to be able to afford new books. As a matter of fact, I'm still too young to be able to afford many new books. Humbled, I learned to enter those mildew-scented, poorly lit palaces of instant gratification, the kinds of stores that would now and then have leather-bound editions of the classics with perhaps water stains on their uncut pages. Water stain, watermark, how was I to know the difference? I was into leather-bound editions of the classics by age 15.

It wasn't until I went to college, though, that I really learned to indulge myself. I had expense money. I also had wheels: I was the only student in the dorms who had brought her bike to college. As I was also the only lesbian in the world, me and my bike continued our exclusive relationship when I wasn't recruiting for the cause.

This all took place in Bridgeport, Connecticut, which turned out to be not a bad place to ride. Flat streets, plenty to see. My memory is actually foggy about Goodwill's exact location, but it was at least in the shadow of one of those Early Barnum edifices. Approaching the store for the first time I felt like a character out of Ali Baba and the Second Hand Thieves. I tethered my trusty two-wheeled steed and strode cavalierly into the den of treasure. (It's real hard to stride cavalierly in Bridgeport. They look at you funny.) I was in luck. The dimly lit cavern was presided over by a genie. At least, she looked kind of like a genie.

The Genie was a very tiny woman with a limp. Of indeterminate age, with ashy-dark skin and tightly-controlled hair, she dressed in what looked like the cream of Goodwill genie coordinates. The counter behind which she was installed was heaped with goods of every description. She suspiciously inspected every person and object that moved into or out of the cave, as if jealously guarding real splendor. I was scared to death of her.

No matter: the front sales room, to me, held nothing but junk (If I could get my hands on some of that junk today! Art deco furniture, antique oak chests, '50s paraphernalia!) I went back to the long hallway, perhaps 60 feet of it, double-lined with floor-to-ceiling books — every shelf holding an unbelievable double row. They held first-edition Willa Cathers, John Steinbecks in original paper editions, perfect Modern Library Classics. Prizes, in other words, to make a budding bibliophile give us lunches for years.

Nor was all of this sheer indulgence. My isolation drove me to desperate measures at college. Whether I missed the last train out of Grand Central and therefore curfew after a night at the bars, or was caught at 4 AM in a hotel room passed out with a girl, I racked up enough of these queer offenses to be referred to a shrink. He did more harm that good peddling "healthy boy-girl relationships" as the solution to my errant ways. He never did figure out the source of my deep depressions. He did, however, share one of his own cures for the blues. "Go down to Goodwill," he instructed me, "and buy some used books." Thus was my second-hand mania legitimized.

The next phase in my thrift-store career was generational. In the mid and late '60s we pinko queer effete snobs created a market for those army surplus items that became our wardrobes. For discarded jewelry that we transformed to love beads. For bedspreads turned into curtains and curtains that metamorphosed into skirts. For faded jeans that became the official uniform.

Army-surplus stores boomed. New second-hand shops opened everywhere with cute names like Second Hand Rose, San Francisco's Purple Heart Thrift Store and Provincetown's Uptown Strutter's Ball. Stores that catered to us displayed new merchandise that looked old. Even today pre-washed jeans command ridiculously high prices.

I shop at the local Penney's only for underwear and gifts. Otherwise, why bother with high-pressure sales people in stores that don't stock what I want? I get tired of mumbling, "It's for my teenage nephew!" or raising eyebrows when I go into the try-on rooms with male apparel. Not to mention the perils of being braless when sales ladies rip open curtains to see how you're doin', dearie. Give me Sally's Boutique any day.

I'm likelier to meet people I know in second-hand shops anyway, people as excited as I am about finding the perfect, long-lusted-after pair of bib overalls. Occasionally I'll get a call from the Neighbor Boys, Bob and Ed, purring over a Fiestaware find, clueing me in on some Bauer bowls with almost no chips at Goodwill. They've built whole sections of their attractive home from discarded windows and doors.

Have gay women and men always been drawn to thrift stores? Because many of us financially need to shop there? Because of our fascination for costuming? Recently I found myself shopping next to two men. I was looking for passable clothing for my job, they for something outrageous for their real lives. In Macy's women's department they could not have had such fun. In a thrift store, even in this fundamentalist town, the straight customers just smiled at their low-key histrionics.

I love our gay culture. It's as comfortable for me as second-hand clothes. We're bold and innovative enough to dip into the straight world's refuse, to salvage not only their unwanted possessions, but their unwanted people: ourselves.

Nude Newspapers and Dyke Dimples

Some weeks ago I made the daily pilgrimage to my mailbox, that brave receptacle of civilization on our lonely rural route. Amongst the guilt trips from the dentist, vet and ObGyn, lay a gay newspaper. Unstapled, without an envelope, limp and accessible to any eye, it sheepishly attempted to secrete itself under my ninety-first invitation to apply for a Citicard.

I looked over my shoulder to see who might have noticed this accusing envoy. It was probably the month's copy of *Sissies Speak Out,* or worse, *Raging Bulldagger Rag.* Even if it was the more discreet *OG&LHQMRPC,* the headlines had done me in with the postal service. *Transvestites To Bestow Lavender Robes On Pope. Dykes On Horses Rout Rangers' Bar Raid. Gay Teacher Wins Right To Use* Sapphistry *As Sex Ed Text.*

One would think the publication of lesbian books would help lay my fears to rest. Surely The World knows about me by now. Not so. The World doesn't frequent our kind of bookstores. The World is not on Naiad Press' mailing list. The World much prefers to keep its nose out of what it can't handle. It sleeps better at night when it ignores us prowling through its moral bushes. What can I say? I get paranoid easily.

Sometimes, of course, it's not paranoia at all, but good healthy self-defense, survival tactics, a wall of sanity against an insane world that would hurt us for simply loving one another. It doesn't make a bit of sense to me. Can it to them? Perhaps we queers touch a deep-seated fear of underpopulation in enormous numbers of heterosexuals. I sure wish they'd get over themselves. I'd love to feel comfortable when I receive envelopes stamped *Dykes Against Nuclear Technology,* or postcards exhorting me to *Elect A Dyke For President.* I would have loved to shout in joy when a woman approached me at a business meeting for my straight job and asked, "Do you happen to know a book called *Toothpick House?*" How could I get out of that one when my picture is plastered across the back cover and my name across the front? But I was in luck that time. The woman was a lesbian, her approach simply a signal.

And it's signals which are the other side of the paranoia coin. *Bulldagger Rag's* arrival, undisguised, may have threatened my well-being in this community of tight-assed fundamentalists whose hobby seems to be circling the local Planned Parenthood office like famished buzzards; my co-worker's question may have given me a bad moment — but there's no way I would choose to live without either. I wouldn't have them if such risky ventures, which I'll call signaling, though of very different types, were not attempted.

Though I began a recent Northern California trip with Girlfriend intending to document for this column incidents of paranoia as we stopped in motels, visited tourist spots and spent most of our time in public, I found that it wasn't the paranoia, but the moments of positive connection which demanded my attention.

At Lassen State Park, for example, there we were, on a volcanic mountainside, the stench of sulphur steaming at us from a thermal area, mud bubbling and seething all around. Two slender young men with *that look* about them followed us from the parking lot. The area was empty of people except for we two couples. There was no doubt that these men were compatriots, but how to make that contact?

We exchanged pleasantries with them. Quick-thinking Girlfriend, in naming our small town, identified it by saying *RFD* (the rural gay male magazine) had once been based there.

"Oh!" said one of the men, stretching the word impossibly into two emphatic syllables. Boyfriend, on the other side of their car, nodded, beaming, until I thought his teeth would fall out.

What made us want to cement this unexpected affirming connection in the wilderness? Why did we have to let them know, need for them to tell us in some way? Why now, as I tape this, driving through a small Western city, do I smile to see the two older men, obviously tourists, who walk motel row with gold chains around their necks and an infinitesimal sway to their hips? Why do I want to toot my horn in welcome?

There is a charm to this underground life of ours. At times it seems that our subculture, flourishing for centuries, is no longer needed, what with gay liberation and all. But if it should outlive its purpose, if life gets happier and easier in the open, I'd certainly miss the blend of fear and boldness that goes into our signaling, the sense of flapping wings, of charged air as we circle one another yearning to give greetings.

I remember studying the language of lesbians. Learning to give The Look while barely meeting another dyke's eyes, as if one half of the face must deadpan and deny, while the other confesses and boasts. There would be a narrowing of one eye, a certain drawing up of one side of my mouth into what was more grimace than smile at first. With practice, I got my eye to twinkle with suppressed amusement. My head could nod so slightly no straight would swear it moved. And my left cheek would form a dimple: tough, brusque, amused, hungry — the dyke dimple. *You are not alone. Tell me I am not alone.*

Will all this be lost in our new found freedom? More and more I'm stopped by open smiles in strange places, by women starting conversations at the slightest excuse.

On my way home from North Carolina once, I was settled in my seat on a DC10. Down the aisle came a woman with short grey hair, round glasses, slacks. Respectable-looking, but there was something in the way she moved — I labeled her a Probable. We were, after all, headed for San Francisco. Previous such airborne encounters had prepared me for her to take the window seat by my side. The irrepressible Universe at work again,

102

bubbling hot dykes out of the sky, instead of gay men out of volcanic mud.

We made very brief conversation before our signaling became more sophisticated.

"Do you know so and so?"

"Well, yes! And do you know her — uh —"

Within five minutes I knew she was a PhD who'd taken up teaching like a mission to open her male dominated field to other women. Within ten minutes she knew why my name sounded familiar. We'd both at least heard of each other's lovers. We, in fact, shared a whole local community. I'd found, as my high school gym teacher would have said, another member of the club.

So you see, I'd begun naming incidents of paranoia, and I ended by finding far more moments in which consciousness of my lesbianism led me to considerably more positive experiences.

Signals. Symbols. I Know You Know bumperstickers. Pink proud triangles. Pinky rings. Green on Thursday. Certain clothing, hairstyles, glasses. The Walk. How do we learn it all — *do* we learn it? Is there something inherent in our same sex intimacy that brands us? For years I longed to "look like a dyke." I was over thirty before I was satisfied with the extent to which photographs revealed the-dyke-in-me. Was it fifteen years of studied posing which showed, an accumulation of well-learned gestures and movements? Had the battering of a hostile society, the survival tactic of chemical abuse, left scars imbedded in my very flesh? Do the suffering of oppression and the joy of variant sexuality combine to shape our faces as well as our destinies? Such a bittersweet process, this becoming ourselves.

I want nothing less than liberation for us, nothing more than the simple, unthreatening delivery of a nude newspaper. Yet I treasure The Look, the signal dances, the dyke dimples. If the generation coming out now won't need all the difficult trappings of my era, how will I know them? What will guppies look like at sixty?

Missing the March

The March on Washington took place, for me, in my heart.

I'd been in D.C. the weekend before, so felt as if I'd been part of the preparatory madness. Looking back, I realized I was there before the first March, too. Then, I'd heard a great deal from warring factions: the city of Washington was doing just fine without busloads of strangers pouring in to freak out the local politicians. This time I heard not a breath of this kind of fearful resentment, bred by lack of confidence. It was just plain excitement and manic pre-demo jitters: have we done enough, have we got time enough, ARE WE READY THIS TIME?

They were, all of us were. I was back in Oregon when the first news reports came over National Public Radio. I had my little walkperson clipped to my fatigues, my headphones snug against my ears as I watered Girlfriend's incipient, still potted, palm and eucalyptus forest. Girlfriend was in Washington marching. Under her young thirsty fronds I was crying. Crying at all those beautiful gay people getting married like we did last year; crying at the brave enormity of the procession itself; crying at the arrests outside the Supreme Court. I cried especially over the AIDS quilt interviews: a monument the size of two football fields and, tragically, growing. Giving a spicy eucalyptus an extra dousing in celebration of life, I thought, we sure have emerged from the shadows and learned to take up our space.

I'd wondered how straight America was reacting to this many-headed queer monster prancing, or stomping, through the capitol. Later in the week the local paper ran this AP report: *The Senate voted overwhelmingly Wednesday to deny federal money for AIDS education materials that critics say promote homosexuality.* On NPR, conservative senator Jesse Helms, instrumental in this vote, was quoted after he'd examined safe sex comics produced by the Gay Men's Health Crisis Center of New York. He said, "I almost threw up."

I wanted instant replay of the March after his words, a march bigger and more outrageous, louder and more demanding, once a week until so-called humans like Helms were vomited out of office. I mean, what do these conservative breeders *think*? That *we're* bred on another

106

planet and imported to offend them? Jesse Helms, we are your daughter, your son, your cousin, neighbor and your co-worker. We are your minister and your grocery clerk doing it together, your teachers and the people who write the songs, who make the films that move you. What shook you up so much about your sexuality that you cannot even look at graphics of men making love?

My anger took me back to an office where I used to work on the East Coast. I had become very close to a gay man (are you out there, Vipe? Are you alive still in this war against sexual enlightenment?). We used to talk about everything under the sun — or under the fluorescent office lights. One day the odd subject of heterosexuality came up. "*I* think it's perverse," Vipe whispered, "what they *do* together." "Wow!" I cried, at the risk of losing our jobs. It was the first time I'd ever heard another person say my feeling out loud. To me, female-male sex is very queer. I was never convinced until recently that people really do enjoy it. I think it's great that they do, but they can have it. Meanwhile, I'm healthy enough, and secure enough in my own sexuality that visuals of such lovemaking do not make me barf. Good thing. They are everywhere.

As we were everywhere in Washington. I would have loved to have been able to march with Girlfriend, but I'm humble: I'll settle for having been in the vanguard.

I was asked to D.C. by Lammas Bookstore and a community group called Brother Help Thyself. Both Lammas and Lambda Rising bookstores scheduled a series of readings; Brother held a dinner to honor gay writers. The latter was given at the Meridian House International. Now, you all know how difficult it is to outclass dykes in dykey clothes and backpacks. But this dive managed. There we were. Debbbie Morris, manager of Lammas

107

Dupont Circle, and Mary Farmer, Lammas owner, and me, trudging up imperial-palace-style wide marble stairs under chandeliers and ancient tapestries. It didn't get any easier. All around were guys in evening wear amongst the ornate antique furniture. I felt as if I was in the apex of Washington Society. As if Jesse Helms would feel more comfortable there than me. Until, that is, I started talking to some of the guys. Like Cornelius from Brother. He charmed me into feeling comfortable. Or David with his cowboy boot fable. Or John, the waiter, hovering like a devoted den mother. I think I could get used to that kind of style. If they still let me wear my dungarees and backpack.

My original '79 trip to Washington was a chance to meet, in person after about twelve years of correspondence, Barbara Grier, one of the four founders of Naiad Press. I also met Donna McBride that weekend, another of the four. Imagine my surprise this year when the other two founders, Anyda Marchant and Muriel Crawford, appeared at my reading. You could have knocked me over with a drag star's feather boa. Once more I was charmed, this time by these two farsighted members of our older generation who have given lesbians so much.

Right after my reading, Ann Allen Shockley, author of *Say Jesus and Come to Me, The Black and White of It,* et. al., arrived to sign books. Small and sprightly, with an air of sharp understated intellect, Ann Shockley is one of the most accomplished of this generation of feminist writers.

It's always gratifying to spend time with other writers. My contact with Shockley was brief, but I was able to hang out with Becky Birtha for almost twenty-four hours. I'd liked the stories in her first book, *For Nights Like This One, Stories of Loving Women,* but

108

her work felt as untried as I knew mine was. With her new volume, *Lovers' Choice* (SEAL), I am very sure of her talent and skills. Her prose is soft-spoken, almost plain, but its light is bedazzling, shining on and enlightening my life and the lives of the women I see around me. In person she is soft-spoken, too, appearing serious and delighted by turns, with the brightest sparkle in her eyes that I have ever seen.

It is said that art lays the groundwork for revolution. Did this cultural weekend presage the March?

I suspect, Mr. Helms, that you may also have been reacting to our March when you experienced your desire to belch forth the contents of your system. Just think! Half a million strong though we were, Becky and me, Muriel and Anyda, and who knows how many others had already gone, or never left, home. Contemplate, sir, the unsleeping mountain that we are, whose spirit invades those hallowed streets, always. You can insult our work, disdain our presence, but you can't still the marching in our hearts.

Taking On the Bigoted Beast

Going to the post office in southern Oregon can be radicalizing. I was innocently running up the steps last month when I noticed a little man sitting at the top. Between us was a table — and a huge sign that read *NO SPECIAL RIGHTS FOR HOMOSEXUALS.*

Like a tidal wave, rage swallowed me. I kept moving toward him. My mind scrambled and unscrambled itself in a frantic search for words. I have always been unable to vent my anger aloud. Pictures came: Me tipping the table

110

over onto him. Me ripping the sign down. Me shattering him with kicks. Me being wrestled into a police car, my ability to earn a living or even live in this county with my lover destroyed. Him self-righteous, virtuous, a *Christian* martyr. And all for two lines about my disorderly conduct in the local police column.

I should explain. Neil Goldschmidt ran for the governorship of Oregon promising to issue an executive order banning state agencies from discriminating on the basis of sexual orientation. According to *Just Out* editor Jay Brown, "A clause in the executive order clearly prohibits affirmative action or preference for homosexuals in state employment." It seemed, in other words, a harmless order.

Last October, Gov. Goldschmidt, probably well aware that the state is rife with queers and our liberal friends, did as he promised. The state is also rife with Christian fundamentalists and conservatives. And these bad guys, who would prefer to exterminate us if they just could, found an excuse to harass us. They want to petition away the governor's harmless work.

The little man at the top of the post office steps — I use the term *little* in its spiritual sense — was collecting signatures to this end. He only needed 63,578 to place the measure on a general election ballot.

Later I learned that Girlfriend had engaged the man verbally. Though he was curiously unresponsive to her, another man took up the cause, and when she left he was still haranguing the little man. Meanwhile, Girlfriend was bearing down on the postal officials, who also proved curiously unresponsive to her complaint about being accosted for offensive causes.

Later still I drafted my letter of thanks to the governor. Then I scrounged up the cash to pay my dues to the Gay and Lesbian Press Association, and I joined Galon, a tiny group in a small city nearby, and the Lesbian Community Project, a larger, highly political group in Portland. Next I shall write to the postal officials. I decided to march this year in the Portland Lesbian and Gay Pride parade come hell or high water. I am writing this column, which should reach thousands more people than the little man and his counterparts ever will. And my anger and my commitment will burn on and on.

Why did this particular incident get to me? After all, the day before the powers that be in D.C. had voted a huge AIDS package. Why ain't I grateful?

Because nothing has essentially changed. Are we so used to living in fear and with great caution that it feels normal to us?

I came out in 1960 when telling one's parents was unthinkable. When there were two gay organizations, not hundreds. When there were two periodicals, and the few books published were for prurience, not politics. When the only gay parades were the half-tanked groups boisterously strutting onto gay beaches or the lines of singles and couples nervously straggling past a bouncer into the bars night after night after night. One becomes used to the undercurrent of oppression. I'm not sure I know how to function without it.

Living in a time that often feels like the not-so-old days reminds me how tenuous our victories really are. It keeps me working when I'd rather rest and look back at how far we've come rather than ahead at how far we must go. It keeps me aware that although we edge toward deep changes, only we can make them. Only Girlfriend, taking on the bigoted beast in public. Or me, running home to write checks and scribble my protest. Even with all the good straight women and men in the world, no one is going to do it for us. We are not too sick, too weak, too deranged or too liberated. We *are* still too scared.

We look back to our predecessors and think of how brave they were — but so are we. We forget how vulnerable we are. I didn't think of it as courage when I wore my dyke finery back then, or held my lover's hand on the street. I worried, yes, I worried all the time. Still, I grabbed every opportunity I could to be in a place where I could dress as I pleased and hold her hand. When I escaped for a moment from the feeling of fear, it was the act I undertook that absorbed me, not the nobility of my deed in the eyes of history. Yet those were and are dangerous acts.

I'm nervous walking down the street now. I see myself as obviously gay, and if I'm not obvious, sometimes the person I'm with is. Maybe I'm wearing a pink triangle, or trying to think of a way to explain the double bed I share with Girlfriend. Maybe I'm scared to say where I live, or with whom, or maybe there is a gang of kids ahead and I automatically cross the street, not even aware I've done it.

Now we have more places to go and can easily be with our own. We have cultural supports that enhance our condition enormously. Our politicians and our allies have been able to enact a little legislation here and there. But how much has that changed the everyday struggle of being gay in a straight world? I still takes guts to hold hands with your lover, whether you're on Christopher Street or Main Street. And if I'm not aware of the danger, I'm reckless. And if I'm not aware that I have the power to change the way the world sees that act, I am discounting myself.

Oh, the little man on his postal mountain was a small incident. Still, how many small incidents are happening all the time — and who does he represent? There are people out there who, unbelievably, think we are intrinsically evil. They fear us and will protect themselves against us any way they can: Legislatively, through the likes of Jesse Helms. En masse, through their ignorant petitions that have enormous power. Individually, through queer bashing, tire slashing and just plain intimidation. Most destructively, through the homophobic doubts their attacks inevitably stir up in ourselves. And this will go on until the little men and the little women are shown that they are wrong. We are the only ones who can show them.

Before walking up the post office steps I may have thought the local organizations were molehills in the mountains of Oregon — like me, too small to do any good. But like the little man, they have their counterparts in every other city. I am one wee lesbian writer swinging my pen like a cudgel, raging the only way I know how: to action through words. Every action spreads enlightenment. The people who fight us see through their shadowy fears. They are not likely to step into the light to learn anything. We must step out.

In this month of gay pride I exhort you and I join you — in signing up for the groups and in signing the checks, in writing the books and in writing the petitions, in holding the meetings and holding the hands that hold up the banners that spread across the world and wrap us all into one people, one brave, scared, angry people who marched so strongly on Washington last fall — and cannot stop marching now.

PORTRAITS

A Feeling of Lonely Strength

I am awed by the western United States. When I drove across the country for the first time in 1984, at age 39, I fell in love with the West, especially the mythical desert. Early in March of this year I returned to Arizona, half, I suppose, to reassure myself that it was really there.

I am happy to announce that it was, though in Tucson, my base of operations, there were times only the plentiful palm trees and landscaped cactuses convinced me of that. The city looks as though it is owned by a concrete conglomerate that pours night and day and then pours some more. Around the outskirts of this island of cement, though, are the saguaro cactuses, the palo verde trees, the ocotillos that make the landscape magic.

And Tucson draws magical people to it. I was able to spend time with two of them.

Valerie Taylor's been in town for some years now. She's been on the lesbian literary scene a lot longer: *Whisper Their Love* (1957), *The Girls in 3-B* (1959), *Unlike Others, Return to Lesbos* and *A World Without Men* (1963). *Stranger On Lesbos* (1960), and *Journey to Fulfillment* (1964). Naiad Press has reprinted three of these and has published the recent *Love Image* and *Prism*.

In the early 1960s, when I was starving for community and enlightenment, my lover and I read Taylor's books. I imagine that they were handed down, dog-eared, from some Older Lesbian, or that we stumbled on them in a seedy Greenwich Village shop. Did the heroines go straight? The Lesbians end badly? Whatever, those shocking paperbacks set fires in us. We were endlessly curious about the author. *Was* she? What did she look like? Were we likely to meet her in the bars when we were old enough? And would we ever write books about Lesbians, too?

What a thrill to get the still unanswered questions answered in an exotic (to me) desert town. What a thrill to see Valerie Taylor at last, under a starry Western sky, in the doorway of her tiny concrete home. What a thrill to ask her to go out with me on a Saturday night. If anyone had told me, in 1960, that I'd ever ask *Valerie Taylor* out on a *date!*

Valerie is in her seventies now. She's little and dark-eyed and warm and generous and articulate. Back when I was reading her books she had just left her

118

husband and was supporting her three boys by writing and editing. My teen lover and I weren't likely to run into her in the bars, but she was actively a Lesbian. She is still actively a Lesbian for that matter. She is also very busy in the peace movement and with the local Food Bank and I cannot remember all the ways she spends her boundless energies.

In other words, Valerie Taylor turned out to be *better* than I'd fantasized. All I could imagine at fifteen was some swashbuckling lady killer who had all the answers. What I found was a peace-loving feminist who has all the same questions about war and hunger and equality that I do.

Valerie and I went gallery hopping that Saturday night, in and out of the Tucson art throngs. Our companion was Hannah Blue Heron. Musician and writer, Hannah's work was included in *Lesbian Nuns* (Curb & Manahan, Naiad). She is one of the crew who run Womancraft Gallery in downtown Tucson, a large space devoted to women's art and craft work. I'd known Hannah in Oregon when she lived in a one-room cabin deep in the woods. She'd moved to Tucson to help her arthritis. Immediately, she began to build an adobe home with the help of an assortment of women and good old fashioned tools like shovels and her back.

Hannah's long-legged, white-haired, and actually has the aura of her graceful avian namesake. Her home is literally dug out of the ground, her living room a scooped-out bowl whose contents have been shaped into the adobe bricks which became her walls. Her circular roof is a beautiful structure, almost one with the desert. The skylight at the center of the roof is often occupied by her dog, who simply clambers up there from the ground to assume his watching post.

The other dwellings at Adobeland, where Hannah lives, range from elderly travel trailers to two-story cabins, all woman-made. I met the creator of this woman's land, Adobe herself, an intense former physical education teacher from the East Coast. With impressive staying power, and I would assume great tolerance for the vagaries of our community, she has established something permanent and valuable. I also visited with Zana, the poet and artist, and with Lee Lanning, publisher of *Ripening: An Almanac of Lesbian Lore,* an early classic of the women's movement.

But I spent most of my time at Adobeland with Hannah herself, admiring the accomplishment of her home, looking at photographs of its creation, listening to tales of building her life in the desert.

My visiting was done primarily at night. Days I devoted to the desert itself. My excuse for the trip was research for a book that's been in the works for years. One of the characters is Windy Sands, a retired motor vehicle department employee who lives in her own little shantytown of trailers and shacks where she raises miniature cactuses to sell wholesale. Two other characters, women not unlike myself, visit her. One finds herself in the desert: the other gets from it what she needs to go on.

I'd expected to be enchanted; I hadn't expected to fall more in love. There they were, though, the saguaros, tall cactus sentinels of the dry land, majestic and stubborn against the onslaught of people and concrete mixers. There is a feeling, under the naked Southwestern sun, alone but for jackrabbits and birds, cooled by silent breezes, lured on by the flat easy earth — there is a feeling of lonely strength there. One is reduced to a body and a strangely quiet mind in the presence of the simple divinity which is sun and earth, jackrabbit and that miraculously adapted plant, the cactus.

Those enduring women, who may all be incorporated in Windy Sands: Valerie, Hannah, Adobe, remind me of the cactuses. Heartier than drought or oppression, more alive than floods and restrictive laws, they are setting down roots with their hand-built homes and courageous culture. How could baby-dyke me ever have anticipated this? A search that began so long ago in the bars ended in a place I'd never even believed existed: the magical, enduring desert.

Katie Niles, Photographer

Katie Niles was a professional photographer back in Indianapolis when she first saw an ad for the Ovulars, photography workshops held at Rootworks in Southern Oregon. She took some time off from the wedding studio where she worked, got on a bus, and breathed in relief to escape "all my little brides."

It was only at the Ovulars, working with Tee Corinne, Ruth Mountaingrove, JEB and others, that she could get the input she needed about her lesbian photographs.

Three summers and three bus trips later, she left behind her envy of the grooms who got to wear tuxedos and moved all her earthly belongings to the land that had stolen her heart and challenged her considerable talent. After, that is, one last trip to the east coast to see Meg and Chris at Carnegie Hall — in a tux of her own.

Though she'd hoped to get a job doing darkroom work in Grants Pass, near Rootworks, the first opening that came along was in Ashland as a short-order cook. There she is still, enjoying the town's culture, gay residents and her cooking job — for the freedom it gives her to photograph women who aren't at all the marrying kind. Often, she hasn't the money to buy film, but when she has, her photographs, especially her portraits, are among the best in our lesbian culture. Her work can be found in *Blatant Image* 1, 2 and 3, *On Our Backs, Off Our Backs, Womankind* of Indianapolis, *Paid My Dues* of Chicago, and the Crossing Press *Calendars*.

Niles is a preacher's daughter and her father's hobby was photography. She recalls that she and her sister would get instamatics for Christmas as kids. Later, when her father hadn't time to use his darkroom, he turned his daughters loose in it. Though he didn't teach them to use it, by 10 or 11 both girls had taught themselves the rudiments of photography. Niles' major influence right through high school was Imogen Cunningham. By the time she hit college, her skills were so advanced she couldn't bear to waste time sitting through prerequisite photography courses and settled for a teaching degree.

She graduated at that point, from documenting life on the family farm, taking pictures of cats and sheep and scenery, to documenting life on campus. More specifically, to do doing portraits of her women friends. She got so serious she brought her whole darkroom with her.

Eventually, she began to concentrate on portraits of one particular woman. She remembers thinking they were "just real good friends," until, one day . . .

It was after college that Niles began to concentrate on portraits of lesbians. That first lover was a very closeted professional. As Niles found herself getting freer and freer in her lifestyle and her work, they separated. Then, she says, "I realized there's a whole *bunch* of women out there!" Her influences became JEB and Tee Corinne, especially Corinne's "Sinister Wisdom Poster" and Holly Near album cover. Perhaps Niles' most famous photograph is of two black women, clothed, one on the other's lap, turned, almost kissing, touching intimately. It is a powerfully erotic image. (*Blatant Image* I, p. 50.)

Though she can't take as many pictures in Southern Oregon as she did back in Indiana, Niles says her work out here is more consistently good. Living here has its problems, though. It was easier to get to lesbians in the city. Here, we are fewer in number and live farther apart. She doesn't own a car. Still, she sees enough of fellow photographers, she feels, to get much of what she once got from the Ovulars: the feedback, the encouragement, news of the lesbian photography market.

Her goals are as clear and down to earth as she is: to make enough money this year to buy more than one roll of film at a time, to afford other materials she needs. Niles is not discouraged, though. There's enough time left, she says, to accomplish her long-term goal: "To be Imogen Cunningham at 92 and still going!"

Mean Norma Jean

Norma Jean Coleman is in her sixties. Her eyes twinkle, she's as slender and lithe as many thirty-year-olds. Her humor is irrepressible, her home the product of ambition and energy beyond anything of which I'm capable. She good-humoredly refers to herself as Mean Norma Jean — and strikes a menacing pose which dissolves to a shy delighted smile every time.

Mean Norma Jean's trailer was one of the few places one could go to get warm at the Twelfth Annual

Womansource Fall Gathering, organized by volunteers from Ashland's women's organization. It's a small, homespun kind of festival, just made for locals like Norma Jean and me, but so rich in its flavor and offerings, women traveled from Vancouver and Arizona to enjoy it.

Jill Macy was the Fall Gathering's heart this year. A small, red-haired and cheery social services worker in real life, she used her skills to round up a host of volunteers who organized everything from entertainment to workshops to full-time nurses. Claire Indigo and Eileen, of Michigan Women's Music Festival renown, make an art of cooking for hordes with an all-volunteer staff. I love working in their kitchen as much as eating their healthy, but sinful, desserts. After Michigan, with its thousands of festival-goers, they call the Fall Gathering fun.

And it was. Despite three days of rain. It's surprising how dry even Birkenstocks can stay on the floor of the great pine forest where the Gathering is held. Nights were heated only by cuddling with a lover or friend. There were complaints of leaky tents from those who hadn't passed to Norma Jean's state of the art camping. And cold water outdoor showers weren't exactly reasonable in the chill damp morning air.

But the camaraderie, the connecting, the talents and knowledge kept us captive. Among the workshops were Tai Chi with Hawk Madrone, Bearded Women, Working in the Belly of the Beast (straight jobs), Being "Single," Adult Children of Alcoholics, a Butch/Femme workshop, Getting in Touch With Your Chakras with Hannah Blue Heron and One Woman's Journey Toward Healing. All weekend, AA and Al-Anon Workshops were available.

I sat ensconced at the Craft Exhibit next to Hawk Madrone, who sold her nature photographs and took orders for knitted socks I longed for all the cold day.

126

Women sold art work, the ever-present tiny bags on strings, jewelry, herbs, tapes, and T-shirts. Yael from *Eugene's Women's Press* publicized the paper while Debra of Grants Pass gave non-stop haircuts. A seller on the other side of me had attempted to ride her horse to the Gathering, but hadn't realized what a slow trek it would be, and returned home for a car full of horsepower. The traditional auctioneer collected an offering from each of us to raise funds for Womansource. Norma Jean showed up, bright-eyed, to buy one of my books and bear it like a trophy through the milling crowds.

Friday night there was a dance. And before it, Annie and Amy taught folk dancing to laughing, tripping, enthusiastic students. The dance was held in the old wooden lodge and the band, Honey Bee and the Stingers, was perfect for an evening's romp. Girlfriend and I danced next to young Nathan and his mother Gail. I only hope I did the music as much justice as Nathan did. Boy children raised in an atmosphere that includes Fall Gatherings will surely help to change the world.

Gail was one of the entertainers in the Personal Theater group from Flyaway Home. Her piece was bout mothering a boy child in our community. Hawk Madrone introduced the evening's fare with a hearty ringing voice that managed to wrench tears and laughter from the enthusiastic audience. Bethroot, sequined and scaled, acted her Laurel Tree Myth. Carolyn Myers, formerly of the Lillith Theater in San Francisco, performed "Tales of Aging and Beyond."

Norma Jean was certainly one of my most important connections this year and she invited some of us to her home soon after the Gathering. With her two dogs circling and leading, we toured her land on well-worn paths. At one end was The Silly Tree, an "L-"shaped madrone on a

127

stilt, and at the other a large, organized workshop full of souvenirs from Alaska and the crafts she'd made with her late lover. After an incredible salmon dinner (she's a devoted fisherwoman, though the salmon was not her fish story) we settled down to pore over albums full of scenes from her life. Mean Norma Jean looks slightly more like her nickname on a three-wheel commercial motorcycle doing delivery work in full uniform — including pants — in the 1940s. An older Norma Jean as a successful Alaskan businesswoman poses with homes she and her lover built. And Norma Jean the sailor, proudly displays the lovers of her youth. She told tales of travel and hunting and baseball —

The baseball took me back a month, to another evening of gathering. Girlfriend had invited Scottie down from Roseburg. While Norma Jean had been pitcher on an amateur team in Alaska, Scottie had been a second-basewoman with the short-lived, but highly popular Women's Professional Baseball League. During World War II the men were fighting, and the baseball fans were hungry. Wrigley, of men's baseball fame, organized a league of women.

Scottie told us how she'd grown up near Chicago and played ball as a girl, then heard of this league and tried out. She was good enough to get paid for it. The teams would play packed bleachers in small towns, men as well as women cheering them on. History tells us about Rosie the Riveter, but not of Scottie the Second Basewoman. Hell, I thought Joanie Joyce invented league ball playing for women with the National Women's Professional Softball League in the late 1970s. Now I want others to know about these sportswomen of the forties. Is there a fan out there eager for a woman's sports herstory project?

Scottie lives in Southern Oregon now, having migrated here after following the Southern California ballplayers home when the war ended. How many Scotties, Norma Jeans, are out there? They make me want huge Gatherings that reach them and bring them to me, to all of us, to be quizzed till we've filled in some of the gaps of our past — and to be honored.

Akia

The second day of February. Southern Oregon a crazy mix of snow and wild violets. Of closed roads and snowdrops glistening in the sun at four in the afternoon, their finally melted frost like dawn dew. Lesbians in their winter doldrums stretching, yawning, peering out of cozy homes, wishing for spring, wishing for excitement, wishing for the bare-chested days of summer. Valentines Day is still weeks away and with it Roseburg's Sweetheart Ball, Ashland's Heart-breakers' Ball and The Dyketones.

We stretch our dancing muscles under warm electric blankets, limber up on our lands for the growing season.

Hungry for culture I planned to travel to Roseburg the other night to see the film *Querelle*. If it's not about dykes, at least it's based on a book by Jean Genet whose magical but sometimes gruesome fantasies of variant sexuality I find strangely insightful. Like Djuna Barnes, or later, John Rechy, he depicts sexuality as an affirmation of life, a transcendence of death through eroticism.

But snow kept me from my affirmation. And it was a lesbian, appropriately, who helped me find it another way.

Like trumpets the dyke telephones of Southern Oregon rang out. Someone was having a potluck! Like armies from heaven the lavender hordes stirred, preened, tried to contain their dancing hearts. That Saturday night the love that dares not speak its name, heavily cloaked, chains on its tires, took its first sleepy steps out of hibernation toward spring.

Thirty-six women! Thirty-five lesbians and a lone brave straight woman packed into one house whose roof, I would swear, began to tremble at our energy. One was from Portland, several from L.A. via Womanshare, one from Coquille. But most were from a main trunk of the Amazon Trail, I-5 between Ashland, Oregon and Roseburg, driving well into the night just to be together. We stretched a collective stretch and told one another our stories, shared our plans, admitted our talents. One visitor was Akia, a local singer-songwriter whose story is typical of what these southern woods harbor.

Akia is a handsome redhead, able to charm audiences, whose career spans from a sojourn as a "girl singer" with an otherwise all-male big band to her presently prolific

131

compositions of songs about women-loving-women. I was pleasantly surprised to hear the big band influence in the soft romance of her lesbian lyrics, in her slow dance lyrics. I've seen her in action, have, as a matter of fact, a tape she made, and find her voice seductive, as pleasing as anyone on the Olivia label. Her lyrics are smooth and have the makings of popular lesbian songs. Even her song titles sing — like: "Is It Love or Is It Lust?"

She's living in the country, a mile up a dirt road, without neighbors, in an unfinished house she smilingly considers a training ground for handywoman skills. Her room is a trailer outside where she retreats to make space for herself and her lover, also a musician. She composes inside, though, with guitar or piano, in doorless rooms, under insulated, but exposed, ceilings. That's typical Southern Oregon dyke architecture; high energies and creativity seem to thrive in it.

I first heard Akia at Womansource's Fall Gathering. She sat on a rock in the full sunlight, guitar on her lap, and seemed to capture that brightness in her liquid alto. Later, she told me she learned to sing around campfires. As a matter of fact, she gratefully blames "everything I am" on the Girl Scouts. She began to write songs in Oregon, after leaving college in Illinois. For a year and a half she sang professionally, in restaurants, and in coffeehouses like Mountain Moving Cafe in Portland.

She tells a story of her two and a half years in the big band — where vocalists were not highly regarded by band members, so she claimed to play the trumpet. In actuality she'd only played french horn and that not for ten years. But she proceeded to prove herself in the second trumpet chair. Grudgingly, the boys in the band came to respect "their canary." And she found acceptance there too, for the first time, for her mellow voice. All her life she'd been urged to "sing like a girl."

Akia's voice gets somber, her eyes angry when she talks about how hard it is to be heard, to even get a dinner house booking when she's real. Her songs are about her life, about our lesbian lives. Though she's given up worrying that she'll lose straight jobs, she listens when the women in her life express fear for their own safety through association with her — and is silent.

Still, she finds music the major healing agent in her life, writing to "do something" with all the emotions inside her. She relaxes to Portland's own Musica Femina and to the Windham Hill artists. Her name is becoming familiar at music festivals.

Akia didn't sing at that Saturday night gathering. Didn't have to in that room full of the plain song of lesbian lives. But she might have sung. I heard her lyrics, an undercurrent of affirmation like a rushing spring creek given words:

> I only write songs when I'm down,
> 'Cause then I stop and think of all the joy I
>   have found:
> The crazy people I know, and all the love they let
>   show —
> I say how can a body stay down, down, down . . . *

*Copyright 1985, by Akia.

133

Georgia

The Oregon coast is something that I, a native Easterner, could not have imagined. Maine was my idea of wet and wild. Oregon is a giant unending Maine. I'll never forget the day Girlfriend walked me along the beach for the first time.

We were alone — not just on a small patch of sand, with overpopulated beach blankets surrounding us and small humans upending solid pail-shapes. No, we were utterly alone except for a very occasional dogwalker. I had not thought this kind of solitude on a shore possible in the twentieth century. We walked and walked along the water. Waves which the stormiest day on the East Coast could not produce, rose under the sun like a sprinting Niagara Falls, broke, and flung themselves at us.

Girlfriend seemed to be heading in the direction of enormous towering rocks. Not the piles of boulders to be found on the New England coast, but huge single rocks caressed, pounded and shaped by the surf. Closer and closer we got to the amazing prehistoric souvenirs.

And then I saw what Girlfriend had really brought me for. There were holes in these rocks. No, not holes: archways, doors, stand-up caves! The magnificence of nature's work was staggering and miraculous to me.

Afterwards, and yes, it was like after lovemaking, we returned to Georgia's. Her cavern is a small home pitched atop a grassy, gorse-thick cliff from which she could watch the two of us cavort and explore. She encourages her guests to walk the beach she scans by eye from her sedentary aerie. She claims vicarious pleasure from watching those of us under age 80 who can't seem to get enough of the pretty stones and shells, bleached wood and flotsam strewn in the vast natural toy department of the beach.

Georgia already has the pick of the briny crop inside her home — almost a user-friendly gallery. Bowls of jaspers, agates and woods collected and polished when this was her hobby with Jeannie, her late companion. Round blue and green glass balls that once served to buoy nets. A plethora of favored ocean booty. No matter how often I visit, there are always more surprises.

This treasure trove would be enough to draw me back month after month. I suspect, though, that it is Georgia's other loves, art and literature, that hold the most allure for me, and the generous and eager manner in which Georgia shares the gathering of a lifetime.

You see, I've never known anyone like Georgia before. The whole world predicted tragedy for me and my ilk by age 80: we could only be alone, spurned, twisted, bitter, wasted. As a matter of fact, those words fit the youth and middle age predicted for us, too. Now that I have family — generations of peers — I see before my eyes my bright future in the guise of Georgia.

She was born in Maxwell, Iowa, in 1907 — on Guy Fawkes Day, as she is wont to add. She graduated from Rockford College in 1930 and four years later met Jeannie, who had earned an MA from Northwestern. They spent half of 1937 in Europe. Then they lived in Montana for about twenty years, where they earned their living as teachers and proprietors of a little bookshop. Georgia taught modern European history to Air Corps cadets during World War II, Jeannie taught military English to the Army engineers. Jeannie always wrote poetry and was published in some of the finest magazines. Posthumously, Georgia published a volume of Jeannie's verse.

It was in the 1950s that the two lifelong companions came to Bandon, Oregon, for a vacation. By 1958 they'd built their cliff home — and a tiny restaurant where, while Georgia took care of the customers, Jeannie turned out kettles of barbecue sauce for chicken. She also was famous for her ham-on-a-bun sandwiches. The editor (Georgia had accepted a job at Oregon State University Press) and the English teacher settled into a life most married couples only dream about.

Meanwhile, they were amassing collections of books and prints. I have only to mention Utrillo, say, or Bernard

Buffet, or the artist-of-Georgia's-eye, Georgia O'Keefe, to send Georgia, in her wheelchair, on an intensive treasure hunt. She returns with a lapful of art books, or prints, or articles whose subjects range from the Impressionists to Frank Stella.

She gives her memories like gifts, too. One time she told Girlfriend about attending a Chicago performance of Gertrude Stein's *Four Saints in Three Acts* and seeing Gertrude and Alice in the audience.

Another time, on learning of my passion for art depicting New York City, she trotted out a postcard of the city, written to Jeannie by poet and anthologist Oscar Williams. I was flabbergasted. Williams was *only* the editor of all the first poetry books I ever owned and pored over. Georgia's causal possession of such an artifact made literary history seem almost down home, something close to my life and about people like me.

Then there is her connection with Doris Lee, a friend from the Chicago days who made a reputation as a primitive artist. The Chicago Art Institute sells holiday cards using one of her paintings, and I recently saw a print at the Portland Art Museum in Oregon.

Each visit ends after Girlfriend and I wend our way back up from the sand, our pockets full of rocks. We spread our stockpiles before Georgia: a bit of a rock hound, an expert. She then identifies each rock and its potential. For years she machine polished these little sculptures of the sea and sold them at their Sea Shop Restaurant. In our parting ritual, Georgia will lift and inspect each stony offering, categorize and grade the lot.

"Ah!" she'll say, "*This* is a good one. It's hard. And look at these lines," she'll add, pointing out streaks of red or gold or patterns. She can spot petrified wood at a glance. I never even knew that one could find such a thing

137

on the beach. My favorite, a gift from Georgia, is a tweedy little stone with a close-set wavy grain in brown-gray and off-white, shaped by the years, polished by Georgia.

On the other hand, when I pick up a clunker, as I often do, she dismisses it with disdain. "That's *just a rock.* A nice rock, but a *rock.*"

This seems very much in character for a connoisseur of twentieth-century culture, my chairside arbiter, a woman living a rich cultural life who is still drawing artists and writers to her salon by the sea.

THE GEOGRAPHY
OF GAY

The West Coast Women's Music and Comedy Festival

I didn't recognize Robin Tyler with nothing but a walkie-talkie on. Consequently, I never got to thank the comedienne-producer for inviting me to read at her brainchild, the West Coast Women's Music and Comedy Festival. My lack of familiarity with mass nudity aside (Girlfriend says I'm the kind of person who doesn't even *see* naked women), I found this festival to be carefully organized, smoothly administered, even — an unexpected bonus — mellow.

Norma Jean had agreed to make the trip with me several months earlier, *before* she bought the twenty-four foot RV that Akia, a day-stage performer from our neck of the woods, called a Hotel. And which another woman enviously referred to as bourgeois. Could this wheeled culprit have contributed to the mellowness of the festival for me? Katherine Forrest, author of *Curious Wine, Daughters of a Coral Dawn,* etc., and her sweetie, seemed to think so when they arrived hot, harried, hungry at the multi-acred summer camp turned lesbian nation. Katherine organized her presentation while we all exchanged notes on the state of our literature and our common culture shock. I'd at least been to the New England Women's Music Retreat its first two years. Katherine, an L.A. city woman, was even newer to the scene.

Getting Norma's mobile oasis to the outskirts of Yosemite where the Festival was held was another sort of adventure. I'd never driven anything larger than a Ford Econo Van — back in 1971. I was less nervous about my presentation than I was about learning to drive a piece of equipment whose dashboard resembled a cockpit. Norma took the gargantuan wheel first while I learned lesson number one before we'd even topped Mt. Ashland: stumbling around inside a moving RV can produce car sickness. I sat and felt the green pallor drain from my dank face.

Lesson number two was simpler: RVs are bigger than subcompacts. If you're going to drive one, you'd better realize that some vindictive soul will have moved every dot from every line on the freeway to someplace you're not expecting them to be. And in case you don't notice, the other cars on the Amazon Trail will set up such a cacophony of honking you'll think you're a migrating duck.

But it was lesson number three I learned best. Do not, under any circumstances, happen to be driving the first time you've ever piloted such an enormous vehicle when you begin the climb toward Yosemite. And if you're dumb enough to find yourself squeezed into one of those too-small, sinuous steep avenues, with the Bekins moving truck that just dropped the piano off at the Main Stage plummeting downhill toward you — do not look to the right, over the cliff, to be certain you have enough room. You don't.

At Groveland I pulled into a parking lot and let Norma pry me, stiff, trembly-kneed, breathless, out of the driver's seat. She'd been grand for someone about to lose her vacation home. Every time I'd lost nerve she'd growled out the command, "Give it hell!" Our ascent to hell was all her achievement.

But the Festival, you ask, what about the Festival? Please understand I was a writer encouraged to make this pilgrimage by a publisher who promised I'd meet lots of fans. I did make it to the Day Stage twice. Once for Pat Bond doing Gertrude Stein, as usual a moving and totally convincing appearance. I always cry at the end and want to rush into her arms sobbing, "Miss Stein, Miss Stein!" and I went back for SDiane Bogus, Bay area poet. I've been a fan of hers ever since I read *Lesbian Hands* in *Common Lives/Lesbian Lives*.

I also visited the Main Stage twice. Theresa Trull's throbbing music lured me briefly to the sidelines where I watched her small figure mesmerize an audience of countless women. The next night I walked over again, this time with Bobbi Weinstock, a gay activist from Virginia whose cruising-femme stories I could have listened to all night. I caught some of Kate Clinton with her and really liked her new routines. Kate, that is, not Bobbi. Though out there under the glittery mountain sky, wrapped inside the energy of those cheering woman-multitudes, I suppose I might have found some of Bobbi's routines as appealing...

"You're a married woman now," my ex-cruising buddy Norma would chastise me. Norma was Best Butch at my wedding to Girlfriend and donned a burgundy tux to earn the title. For this trip I'd had a sweatshirt made for Norma, black, sleeveless, *butchy* as hell, with big red letters that read: ROAD MANAGER. She proudly displayed it to the packed tent at my performance and did a fine job of managing me, if not that unruly precipitous road through the sky.

Other than these forays to the stages I was more likely to be found in the Festival Sponsored Speakers' tent. I heard Katherine Forrest speak of the current trends in lesbian lit. Judy Grahn of the proud gay history she sets forth in *Another Mother Tongue* — did you know there was once a whole tribe of Fairy People, both women and men? Or that the term gay, rather than being a male appellation, goes back to the goddesses? Later that day Del Martin and Phyllis Lyon spoke of becoming older lesbians and talked good sense about rights and strategies in the heterosexist world. I was resting in the RV after my talk when I heard gales of laughter from the tent. I checked the schedule to see which comedienne was on, but it was JoAnn Loulan, author of *Lesbian Sex* and *Lesbian Passion*.

I also hung around the craft area a while, signing books, getting to talk to the festival goers, to Susan and fellow New Yorker Alice Malloy of Mama Bears Bookstore in Oakland. And to Jeffner Allen, author of *Lesbian Philosophy.*

Probably most important to me of all my experiences at WCWM&CF was the time I spent in my own backyard. RV parking has an added attraction. The crowd seemed a little older, a little quieter, a little less festival-attuned, a little more like me. We, it turned out, had parked in a military zone. Behind us were two Korean vets, one from Chicago and still employed by the army, the other also a civilian, but still in charge of an enormous number of military vehicles. The transportation expert, a Captain when on active duty, was fully of Army stories. She had been on the front lines in Korea and seemed both fascinated and repelled by her experiences there. Over and over in her stories I heard a deep warm caring for her sister soldiers and for the Korean women. She lives in the Castro now, surrounded by her Grandma's furniture in an overpriced apartment.

We had a sailor neighbor too, turned dental technician, and she and Norma, also ex-Navy, hung out together. All four servicewomen assured me that, despite the isolation and fear (described eloquently by Pat Bond in the film *Word Is Out*) endured by lesbians in the armed forces, there is no lack of us there.

Our little encampment in the decidedly friendly territory of Yosemite — tents, pickups, campertops, field kitchen — got real homey, with an everyone-pitch-in atmosphere that made the WCWM&CF truly a festival for me. A festival of dykes, a celebration of us in our RVs and mountain tents, in our clothes and out, in our love of music or literature — or just of women, women, women!

The Eastern Trail

I left Oregon to visit family back East and went on to read, in the last few nights of my trip, at three different stops.

On my way to the first reading I visited Rhea Hirschman of Golden Thread Booksellers in New Haven, Connecticut. She hadn't expected me, but plunged into our visit as if starved for lesbian culture. While Valentine, the fluffy white cat from the attached used clothing store, showed off, Rhea escorted me through some classics of lesbian literature: Carolyn Vance's *Pleasure and Danger: Exploring Female Sexuality, Powers of Desire; The Politics of Sexuality* edited by Snitow, et al., the erotic poetry of Olga Broumas, Ruth Geller's lesbian novel *Triangles. Paz* by Camerin Grae and others.

She went on about the talk Deb Edel and Joan Nestle, of the Lesbian Herstory Archives, did in the class she taught at Yale: lesbian sexuality, butch-femme roles, our history. Rhea said it was a powerful discussion which blew away the young, newly gay students who, after it had all sunk in, came back to her with gratitude and new visions of themselves.

My next stop was the Bloodroot Feminist-Vegetarian Restaurant and Bookstore in Bridgeport, Connecticut. The Bloodroot Collective was warm and welcoming, feeding me from recipes out of *The Political Palate* and *The Second Seasonal Political Palate*, their delicious recipe books, before I read. The audience was a mix of brand new dykes, political dykes and a few old gays, but they all seemed pleased and excited by a reading from *The Swashbuckler*, my novel about an old gay stone butch in Greenwich Village in the 1960s.

Then on to New York City where I briefly visited Womanbooks in uptown Manhattan. The salesperson was Lucy who once operated La Papaya, a woman's restaurant in Brooklyn, N.Y. She gave me a message to deliver at my next stop on the Trail, Pandora Bookpeddlers in Englewood, New Jersey. I delivered it to Vivian Shineman, a straight woman who was more interested and supportive of our culture than many dykes are. Her group wanted to talk about lesbian publishing and writing. There are a *lot* of dykes writing out there, building and building lesbian culture till no one will ever be able to hide us again.

147

Vivian graciously drove me back on the controversial and rutted Westside Highway and I treated myself to dinner in a West Coast style natural food restaurant where I planted myself across from two apparently former lovers. They spent their meal catching up on activities of nieces and nephews and old college friends.

I spent the night at The Lesbian Herstory Archives where I ran into Felice Newman sleeping on the couch. She's a publisher of Cleis Press and was in town to sell books at the Women in Psychology Conference. Later, Madeline Davis and Liz Kennedy of the Buffalo Oral History Project arrived. We talked into the night with Deb Edel of the Archives about break-ups and non-monogamy. That seems to be a national topic.

The next morning was International Woman's Day and before I left we celebrated. Jan, a PhD candidate at Columbia who is writing her thesis on a 16th century French woman poet, sang a Cajun-style lesbian song. She's from New Orleans. Then Madeline sang two of *her* songs, one about the Stonewall riots and the roots of gay liberation, the other her "addict song" about being addicted to falling in love with women who are addicts. Leaving the Archives is always difficult as, unlike any other place on earth, it's for *us* and filled with lesbian sculpture, paintings, photographs, clothes, manuscripts, books and on and on.

But I did manage to leave, braving the NYC transportation system to stay for the night with my first lover, Sue Kenler and her 12-year-old daughter Kris, on Long Island in New York. That evening while Kris took her cabbage patch doll Maryellen next door to the sitter's, Susan took me to Alternative Corners, a lesbian book and t-shirt shop in West Hempstead. The theme of the night was again our history. Three of us had come out in 1960 and another in 1942. Everyone else was post-1970. Susan grumbled that the younger women didn't appreciate what we'd gone through, pointing out that one reason so few old gays appeared at lesbian functions was that many had killed themselves because they couldn't take "the life." Others, of course, went straight for the same reason, and still others are too painfully closeted to be seen in a gay bookstore. But we also discussed the exciting contributions of the newer "generation." These are the lesbians whose relative freedom produces the energy to do the work so many of them have begun: on lesbian alcoholism, for example, or lesbian geriatrics. Their Old Dyke Homes may well provide shelter for us all.

Photographer Shelly Glick was there. When we repaired to the local lesbian bar, which serves non-alcoholic beverages and coffee, she showed me some photographs that appeared in *Blatant Image,* a Southern Oregon feminist photography magazine. She was part of the photography Ovulars held at Rootworks in Sunny Valley, Oregon, though she's a native New Yorker.

But Shelly is jumping back on the Amazon Trail to move to Florida. And I, the next morning, said goodbyes to our Eastern Branch and write this now, across the aisle of a DC-10 from two handsome dykes who won't meet my eye, on the great Amazon Trail in the sky. Going home.

Two Way Trail

The Amazon Trail brings me as many gifts as it leads me to. I hadn't expected to be spending December 25 under the potted pine in our rural Oregon cranny with San Francisco guest Susie Bright, editor of *On Our Backs,* and with Honey Lee Cottrell, long-time photographer and filmmaker of lesbian erotica. But there I was, watching the video-present Susie had made of Honey Lee's film on masturbation, *Sweet Dreams.*

Nor had I expected to while away the day watching *Fun With a Sausage,* a playful and wonderfully androgynous spoof; or watching lesbian striptease from San Francisco's Baybrick Inn. But, as I say, there I was, and two stimulating autumn months were thus aptly ended.

The gifting began at a party for my book *Home In Your Hands,* and for *Erotic Interludes,* a short story collection in which Tee Corinne's "The Woman In Love" appears. The party was quiet, attended by local dykes lured from their own mountain lairs to share an evening of culture by the woodstove. One couple, a hairdresser and a medical professional, had managed in their isolation to find only Rita Mae Brown's books. Till the party — where they heard names like Jane Rule for the first time and left with pockets full of lists and arms full of books. How gratifying, to hand someone a lifeline like lesbian literature.

The next weekend I traveled to another rural hub of the dykedom. I'd never seen *Musica Femina* in concert, but a grant from the Oregon Committee for the Humanities allowed Janna MacAuslan, guitarist, and Kristan Aspen, flutist, to travel locally. They've done extensive research on women composers in order to reclaim and perform works lost to silent history.

At this performance, the audience was as packed with lesbian separatists and radical fairies — both of whom abound in the area — as with members of the cultural elite of Roseburg, Oregon. In their innovative costumes, long lacy gowns for the first set, courtly and colorful suits for the last, Musica Femina waged its gentle revolution. Slides shown by Dr. Jane Bowers, author of *Women*

Making Music: The Western Art Tradition, 1150–1950,
brought cheers of recognition from those who know who
really makes women's music.

Also on tour in November was Sarah Schulman,
author of *Girls, Visions and Everything* and *The Sophie
Horowitz Story.* She stayed with us between appearances
in Eugene and Sacramento. I'd expected her to be bright
and ambitious, but not so sweetly shy. She talked of her
upcoming books, one of which became the popular *After
Delores.* Still very young, she's managed, beyond writing
three books, to travel in Europe and hitchhike in Africa.
She supports herself primarily as a waitress in a sleazy
New York dive where, because employees are hard to
come by, she is always assured of work between
adventures.

Had she stayed another week, Sarah would probably
have visited Womanshare, one of the longest-lived of the
Oregon women's land settlements. Its residents wrote the
classic *Country Lesbians* and have been featured in *I
Know You Know.* I'd just finished a new book and wanted
to celebrate, so when the invitation to a birthday party at
Womanshare came, off I went. It was my first visit and I
was a little concerned about being out of my league
politically, but it *was* a party, not a forum. The guests
included a pump jockey turned management, a lot of
artists, an elementary school teacher, a nurse, factory
workers — in other words, a representative slice of
country lesbians.

The party was held in the main building, a
rough-hewn, low-beamed structure with kitchen, living
room and darkroom — only the essentials. Individuals
lived in smaller spaces on the land. I got comfortable when
I noticed the bookcase was no more political in spots than
mine — I curled up on the couch with a gay male romance

by Gordon Merrick. But I was up tapping my feet with the rest of them when the elementary school teacher and her artist lover showed MTV videos. I couldn't resist "Nasty Boys," that vigorous, if tongue-in-cheek, put-down of heterosexual males.

I reached Portland, Oregon the next weekend excited to see that the new *A Woman's Place Bookstore* on Broadway reflects the professionalism and savvy of a maturing women's movement. Spacious, attractively organized, well-stocked, it appears to be a magnet for the Portland community, a great portion of which tracked its muddy running shoes through that afternoon. I was signing books alongside Girlfriend, and kept noticing one young woman who, unsmiling, pored ceaselessly over books near our table.

"This one!" I heard a while later, and looked up to see the same young woman holding *Toothpick House* out for my signature. She'd been shy, but now turned into a warm bubbling soul, eyes shining, eager to talk about her own career. When she left she backed out all the way, grinning, *Toothpick House* against her cheek like a prize. Meeting readers completes the lonely task of writing — warms, as my grandmother would have said, the cockles of my heart.

From the damp of Portland to the palm trees and contrasting holiday lights of San Rafael, California. I made the marathon ten hour drive alone, after having learned that there *are* no cheap motels in Marin County and that I, therefore, couldn't afford to fly. But I got the best deal in town at a raffish establishment run by two men: the Panama Hotel. It consists of at least two older buildings attached by walkways and extensive latticework. The restaurant is a meandering indoor/outdoor affair. The hotel upstairs is more of the same, with rooms decorated in helter-skelter thrift store camp and always topped off by a ceiling fan.

It was a perfect refuge from the high-power, straight-world workshop I'd driven down for, taught by Sarah Lippincott, non-fiction editor of the New Yorker Magazine, and by Orville Schell, a staff writer. For the 600th time in my life, I found myself the only lesbian, and the only out gay, in the world. On this occasion I was trapped in a roomful of writers who publish in such places as Esquire, Mother Jones, Focus San Francisco and the like. I'd been accepted on the basis of two pieces, a review I'd done for the San Francisco Chronicle, and an Amazon Trail column about The American Bookseller's Association — subtitled Gay Press Row. There was no turning back. I took a deep breath and read a piece that spoke of lesbian culture, of our isolation and our erotica. I knew nobody but the Goddess could get me through this one. In the course of the profile I mentioned that its lesbian subject had also once been married. After the instructor praised my writing, the students honed in on what was apparently the crux of the piece for them — was the subject *really* a lesbian? *Surely* she was bisexual. Or didn't she *know* what she was?

"Take what you can and leave the rest," whispered the Goddess with a tap on my shoulder. I did, learning in the course of the workshop that these were my peers, and that I can compete with them for space in high-paying straight publications, even, perhaps, bringing lesbian and gay culture further into the light of day. My poverty, as well as a messianic streak, tempt me. But, oh, it's the shy young woman in the bookstore, grinning backwards all the way out the door, who I want for an audience.

That shy young woman and the rural couple with their armload of books, the pioneers at Womanshare and the separatists and radical fairies, the real Sophies and Frenchies — and the clerk I happened on in a San Rafael bookshop. I was paying for something by Rilke and hadn't even considered looking for gay literature there. The young, bright-cheeked clerk somewhat timidly blurted, "You look just like the author of a book I'm reading."

I raised an eyebrow.

"As a matter of fact," she said, glancing at my check, "you even have the same last name!"

I raised the other eyebrow and asked quietly, "What's the name of the book?" I'd fallen right into the old gay habit of coy back and forth that allows us to guardedly identify one another.

"*Home In Your Hands.*"

When I admitted to being that very author in the flesh, you would have thought the clerk had been a rocket poised for take-off. "This is great!" she shouted repeatedly, flying toward the rear to get her copy. She seemed to career off bookshelves as she went, explaining to all the other clerks who I was, whizzing back to me. "This is great!" Afterwards, she showed me the tiny gay book section she's nurturing like a garden of promises.

What can I say? The Goddess had tapped me on the shoulder once again and said, "Keep up the good work, kid. You're right where you're supposed to be. Traveling the Amazon Trail."

The Geography of Gay:
Part I — The Graduate

I suppose I should be philosophically opposed to any ghetto, to the very concept of a gay ghetto like the Castro or Greenwich Village. But when I hear of a "lesbian neighborhood" or even of two gay guys moving in up the road from me, I am thrilled. I'm more comfortable right here in this one gas station town of mine because I know there *are* two gay guys up the road, *and* two dykes, *and* two more men, and the women coming and going up on the mountain. We're probably well over our 10% quota, but the rednecks haven't caught on because we're spread out. I only have to endure suspicious looks down at the General Store, even though I *always* wear a shirt and a smile. Could it be my tweed cap that tips them off?

Not that hostile stares are new to me. If New Yorkers do it, could I expect less of rural Oregonians and transplanted Californians? It's my impending move onto my lover's land that has me thinking about lesbian and gay geography, and remembering my own multitude of Moves. Why have I wandered so much? Does a search for a place of our own move us on?

My First Apartment was pink. Not the inside walls, but the three-story house itself. Not only that, but the house next door was pink too. Both were owned by Mrs. Lanniman, a majestic boat of a middle-aged woman from the West Indies. Every Saturday morning Mrs. Lanniman would unlock our door and sail in to collect the rent. Which was okay before Carol Lynne and I became lovers. Afterwards . . . Well, nothing could undo the charm of that First Apartment. The home to which I brought my First Cats. I might even have stayed, but Carol had to return to the dorm for her senior year.

I couldn't afford Mrs. Lanniman's prices, anyway, or such invasion of my privacy; nor had it occurred to me to take in a roommate. As far as *I* knew my lover and I were the only queers in Bridgeport, Connecticut — there was no way I could have shared my closet with a straight in those days. So I moved on into the back half of an already meager first floor owned by Nick the grocer. Nick did not appear every Saturday morning. As a matter of fact, he'd been tolerating my bounced checks at his store for years. But there was a problem. This little palace with a view of a gas station, and a barking German Shepherd guard dog for a neighbor, cost me $110 a month. Cheap? Not on my secretary-salary of $65 per week! I pooled food money with Carol and our unenlightened straight friend Dorothy. The arrangement saved me in two ways: not only couldn't I afford to eat, but I couldn't cook and Dorothy could!

When Carol finally left the dorm to join me, we moved into my all-time favorite apartment, but lost Dorothy. Carol couldn't cook either. We still have giggling fits when we remember our gourmet chicken recipe: place chicken breasts in frying pan; smear with lumps of butter; salt and pepper. Turn on burner and smooch. If still unthawed when checked, return to smooching. Discuss whether to turn it. Cut open. Try and recall whether our mothers' chickens had ever been red inside. After two hours throw out and eat Cheerios for dinner. Obviously, some lesbians when growing up are so intent on refusing to learn to cook for their predicted future husbands, we never consider that our partners will have been as stubborn as ourselves!

In any case, Columbia Street, in the heart of an hispanic ghetto, was magical to us. There was a long narrow side yard we affectionately called The Garden of Eden. Weekend nights an older drunken man would sit on a stoop across the street and sing loud Spanish songs. Our friend Walter lived across the hall and visited frequently with us. He particularly enjoyed my naked manikin Myra Breckinridge whom I'd wheeled home from the Goodwill across town on my bicycle. We also had Marty and his girlfriend up the alleyway to visit — if we were in the mood for perpetual Rolling Stones, hallucinogenics and black light posters. Wow, man.

Aside from the toilet and shower in the hallway the apartment's main drawback was a no-pet policy. We thought to elude this by referring to our cats only in code. We called them — no, I don't remember why — Christmas Trees. When we were certain the landlord was at work we'd sneak out to walk the Christmas Trees in the Garden of Eden.

It was while we lived in that apartment that we met our first gay compatriots. I'd begun driving lessons, hoping the $5600 a year from my new state job would allow me to buy the VW of my dreams. (How would I ever meet the payments on the price of a brand new Bug: $2300 including tax and dealer prep!) My first driving instructor was male and by our second lesson he'd asked me out. I must have looked at him like he'd asked me to cook a chicken dinner, because Jane showed up for my third lesson.

Jane Dow. I was in love at first sight. I mean, she was good-lookin', a gay grown-up, and smooth as instant chocolate pudding (Carol and my favorite gourmet dessert). I was so crushed out on her I almost flunked my driving test not because I couldn't parallel park, but because she was in the back seat. She'd explained almost immediately that the other driving teacher was gay, had been sounding me out, and passed me on to Jane when he was sure I was a dyke.

It wasn't long afterwards that we moved from the Garden of Eden to a four-story older apartment building around the corner from Jane's. Not that we saw her much, but the neighborhood glowed with romance because she was near. We learned, then, that like attracts like, even when the likes don't know . . .

A classmate of Carol's moved in downstairs with another woman. Were they? Of course they were. Our excitement was high. We now knew three lesbians. Then a gay man from our school took another apartment in our

159

building. It seemed I couldn't go out in my new blue VW (which used $3.50 in gas a week) without bumping into a gay.

But we had a hard lesson to learn. The presence of queers did not make a community. Though we were separated only by stairways and walls, we remained isolated but for those casual encounters. Our boxlike domiciles were too full of fear. We'd learned to cook a chicken by then, but not to reach out to other people. We'd learned so well to protect ourselves from exposure, and internalized so deeply fear and disdain of ourselves and our kind, that while we sought safety in numbers, it wasn't a feeling of safety we found. We even feared people would notice that we lived in a building full of gays.

Soon after this I moved with Carol to the outskirts of New Haven, a city that boasted a gay restaurant and bar. Perhaps here, we thought, we could find friends. Surely where there were more gays we'd have less trouble connecting. Fascinated, moths drawn to the flame, we'd fled one isolation for another.

We lived in that last apartment together still alone, still lonely for our own, still helpless to give ourselves what we so badly needed. I couldn't figure out why it felt so much better to always watch for signs of gay neighbors, gay co-workers, than to actually get to know them. I didn't understand my ambivalent feelings and continued to listen, for a while, to my fear of running with a telltale crowd.

What a tale of love and fear! Of approach and withdrawal. Of hope and failure. I left the last apartment and my post graduation marriage then. Surely it had been the relationship which kept me wanting, kept me feeling unwhole? I learned differently much later, but not until I, with thousands of other women and gay men in the early

160

seventies, moved on to explore whole new concepts of shelter and community. And kept on moving from place to place in search of a whole healthy self I needed to see, to reflect, to accept.

The Geography of Gay:
Part II — The Collective Phase

Frequent moving had become a generational
phenomenon by 1971, at least for the middle class kids I
knew. When I left the modern balconied apartment I'd
shared with my lover and moved into my own narrow
third floor flat, I was expressing the restlessness of the
highly-mobile baby-boomers, as well as seeking my own
way in life. But this poet-in-a-garret trip was the stuff of

my ancestors; I was destined to live the communal experience of our age to its fullest.

When I hit New Haven that year women drunk on sisterly love whirled in crazed circles at the women-only dances held in church basements. Radical white women did much of the legwork needed for the Black Panther trials. And the first lesbian-feminist living collective was being formed. I and my peers were moving into the Women's Movement.

My first women's dance, after seven years of isolation from gays in and after college, exhilarated me. How did one meet these women? How did a New York butch unlearn the necessarily one-on-one bump and grind and ask two, a dozen, a roomful of women to dance?

As a feminist "old gay" I was a unique addition to the community and didn't have to wait long to learn. Soon after the Gay Women's Group crowded into my living room — which was stuffed with bookcases and otherwise furnished only with a foam pad on the floor and a small rocking chair — I was invited to join that first living collective. There were already at least two daring heterosexual female and male collectives inhabiting ramshackle old homes around town, beginning to found food co-ops, but this would be the only all woman group. Those brave straight women! Risking their reputations and their very sexuality, as it turned out, to live with dykes!

Dykes? That's what they called themselves, but they were strange creatures to me. Highly politicized, adamantly opposed to, for starters: couples, monogamy, exclusive affectional behavior (others might feel left out), and washing dishes; I tried to fit in. But I never got much further than feeling guilty that I wasn't revolutionary enough to relinquish my bourgeois propensity to love one woman at a time, and to show that love not only by helping her do the dishes, but fondling her in very exclusive ways as we worked . . .

All eight of us lived for about $40.00 a month each in a five bedroom house on an exclusive street in the "better" section of New Haven. The neighbors didn't know what to make of our Volkswagen brigade on moving-in day, I'm certain, but were liberal enough not to hassle us.

We began as: Toni, one of the Panther Collective members, dedicated to the revolution, and the kind of hustler who could fundraise a meager living. Bea, a firebrand organizer who shepherded us into collective formation and kept us like that. She was an early mistress of grant writing. Carson, a Yale pre-med student with a musician's dreams. Sara, a straight radical high school teacher who founded one of the country's first alternative high schools. Monica, a mother with her head in the clouds who was dipping into all the worlds she could find after years of marriage. Lillian, her sixteen-year-old daughter, in a constant state of excitement and a pupil of Sara. Goldie, another straight woman, a local who believed in feminism and in living her ideals. And then me. The token old gay. I quit my secure job and went on alcohol, drugs and unemployment, testing the waters of this new freedom, not at all certain I wouldn't drown in my new way of life.

Five women had rooms of their own; I shared mine with my stowaway lover who was finally voted into the collective; two other women shared the basement. This last was a terrible idea as both were members of the New Haven Women's Liberation Rock Band and had to work together in two collectives. I won't, of course, go into who

164

was sleeping or had slept with or would soon sleep with or come out with — who. It would take all day. Suffice it to say that one's room assignment was sometimes fluid.

Except for the diehards in the attic. I can see in retrospect that the sociological patterns of the household were harbingers of our futures, but back then I was simply proud (and guilty at the same time) of the maneuver that allowed Toni and I the luxury of a flight of stairs and an elitist bathroom of our own between us and the others. The others either remained straight or went partly or wholly back to heterosexuality within three years. Toni kept the faith. I met her years later at a Gay Pride March in San Francisco with her girlfriend. And me? Well, there never was any danger that I'd decamp.

For that halcyon radical year, though, we all shared responsibilities of the household and were, maybe, collectively cleaner than the sloppiest of us might have been alone. We *Spent Time Together,* either on individual "Dates" or in group outings (I was always trying to drag the others to gay bars). And we had a weekly housemeeting on Wednesday nights. The words *Wednesday Night* soon took on an ominous tone for me. I was terrible at "Dealing and struggling," much better at withdrawing or forcing humor into deadly serious discussions.

All in all, we worked hard to make a go of our brave new world. Though I felt betrayed by some of the women who laid heavy imperatives on the house only to return to safer waters later, that first collective was a rich and exciting experience. Though I never felt I could be the dyke I was, I could try on other ways of being. And I've always thought, if we did nothing else for the world, at least we helped to desegregate the neighborhood. An

165

Asian family moved in next door while we lived there, and a mixed-race couple bought the house we lived in.

The second collective, an outgrowth of the first to accommodate new blood, was somewhat more relaxed. There were more women in it who had been lesbians longer and who remain lesbians today. Or perhaps it wasn't the gay presence, but a practical need (my primary one at the time) to find a living situation that was cheap and palatable.

The problems in this House were as different as the old house and the new. (A second collective now lived across town.) Possibly because of our longer lesbian history we seemed to have more emotional instability. These women had been fighting for their sexual selves a good long time and did not feel all that comfortable in the world. We had more problems of self-image, economics, family estrangement. To us the liberation and pride movements were lifelines as well as optimistic solutions.

In any case, there were seven of us on two bedraggled floors of a house whose elderly male owner and part-time girlfriend lived and fought on the first floor. We were a motley emotional crew ourselves. The shepherd was with us again, but she was beginning her conversion to a psycho-theory which advocated bisexuality. A sometimes surly local dyke who later found contentment as a foreperson in a coastal fishery had joined us. There was a woman who'd been out as long as me and was as dependent as me on chemical substances. We caused some upset when we announced an attraction to each other and an intention to act on it. The whole House dealt and struggled with that one until the excitement was gone and we retreated. A working class schoolteacher turned band member was possibly the most level-headed of us all. A nineteen-year-old house painter was also in a work collective and struggled on two fronts. Mindy, a sprightly and energetic wanderer, later learned to do light shows at popular discotheques in New York. And I was there again, still, a frustrated writer whose audience had disappeared with *The Ladder* and not yet regrouped. I earned a living as a professional Girl Scout and you can imagine how paranoid that made me.

All four of us in couples had our own rooms. No one lived in an attic or in the basement. All of us were on a pretty equal financial footing. (Income sharing had been big in the first collective, but here there was no longer anything to share.) Our three band members lived in separate rooms. All these things helped the collective be more livable, but probably most helpful was the fact that by this time the thrill had gone. Living as we were was an emotional and economic solution, not a battle in the big war of revolution. I associate the first collective with a New England autumn, leaves brilliantly colored, Yale football crowds cheering at the nearby Yale Bowl, neighborhood children in spanking-new school clothes. At the second house it is always summer in my memory: pushing aside stored dusty furniture to find space for supper on the porch outside the sweltering house, flea-ridden cats and dogs, a jungly backyard.

Then it was over, our enthusiastic young experiment. There was nothing to keep the rest of us together when the other couple moved to Boston. I with my lover the housepainter, found a third floor flat, barely wider than my garret, and began the next series of moves in the opposite direction: financial and emotional stability. Moving was feeling less like an adventure and more like a chore. I'd be moving on, but now, as I neared thirty, it was with an eye toward staying put, putting down roots, nesting, resting, anything but re-moving. And as I slowly but thoroughly severed my ties with the Women's Movement, I entered into a new world, with quite different mating and nesting habits: bar women in a medium-sized city. Here was a whole new lesbian geography to learn.

The Geography of Gay:
Part III — Go West, Young Gay

When I moved into a collective, I moved also into
feminist political activism as I would have into a religious
conversion, but to this day I have no real understanding
of what I was doing beyond saying NO to a patriarchal
world. The experience changed me, but not in a positive
way. I was a non-political beastie in a political age.

I ran, shedding slogan-buttons, from collective living
to return to the exclusivity of coupledom. We took a third

floor flat (lesbians, we agreed, always live on the third floor) in an older home on the Boulevard of New Haven, close to the colleges. I'd returned to the student housing which felt so comfortable to me. But when winter came physical comfort disappeared thanks to a stubbornly frugal landlady who lived on the posher side of town and, through long-winded, self-pitying tales of woe, utterly refused to provide sufficient heat. Both of our cats died there, at least partially from that stress. As if that weren't bad enough, this was also the time of the first gasoline shortage. But it wasn't until *after* my just-paid-off first car (a '70 VW named Lana Cantrell — remember Lana Cantrell?) was stolen, that the police told me three to four VWs were being stolen from the Boulevard each night. Great, I didn't say. Glad you mentioned it. I rented an economy Chevy named Vegala and trudged up and down every street in the city, in a snowstorm, looking for evidence of a VW theft ring. But Lana, like her namesake, had disappeared.

I felt like a victim. This was not helped by being between social groups: still violently allergic to the "libbers," I was not yet integrated into the bars.

But luck, and a fine nose for queerness, had led me, with my lover, to jobs in a convenience store chain whose personnel roster was heavily weighted with gays. One young Phys Ed major, also newly recruited to the chain, began to spend a great deal of time at our house. She'd become my drinking buddy and was to graduate from college in a few weeks. If anything, she seemed more displaced and woebegone than us. Our solution? Moving on, of course, to a bigger, more expensive place — all three of us.

It was a terrible idea. I once did a reading and asked my audience for suggestions for future short stories. One sweet and sad woman in the audience suggested I write about a single living with a couple. She was having a rough time. I think our adopted recruit, though she stayed with us through four moves, may have been as disappointed. For the couple, a threesome was obviously the perfect compromise between the social and economic advantages of group living, and the less debilitating circumstance of individual housing.

We moved all the way around the corner. Why not? The neighborhood was great for long nosy walks past neighbors' homes and for architectural sightseeing. We were close to laundry, drugstore, grocery — and gay bars, listed not in order of importance. My favorite of the bars was a little neighborhood dive called The Parkway, run by an older straight couple. Local straights and gays mixed there. The bartender for ages had been Arthur, a short Italian man given to wearing overlarge rings and long, flowing scarves. Each year he organized a picnic at a State Park south of us, and one year a Thanksgiving dinner which drew a multigenerational crowd and was an experience that made such an impression on me it has appeared and reappeared in my fiction.

Arthur created a sense of community like no one else did in New Haven. Many of the Parkway regulars lived in the red brick apartment buildings surrounding the bar even after he'd left to open his own place. He should have stayed. Perhaps he got too outrageous for whomever controlled bars in that town, perhaps he flirted with danger. Someone rigged his car with a bomb. That didn't get him, but cancer did soon after. Later, I mourned him from my stool by the Parkway door, on a sunny afternoon, watching the street traffic through the open door, playing big band waltzes and "Help Me Make It Through the Night" on the jukebox.

171

The nearness of the bars made that apartment fairly liveable. Our biggest problem was the gypsies downstairs. They were flamboyant, like Arthur, but totally unmindful of those around them. And I was intimidated by their flashing tempers. Sometimes, I'd walk where I was going rather than fight to get their Cadillac out of the driveway where it was blocking Blue, my new red VW. Perhaps I should have identified with them, another downtrodden social group, but the neon sign in their front window advertising some occult fortune-telling service somehow made them very separate from the gay world, though we had similar needs in housing.

So I moved on again. Another convenience store employee ventured to add herself to our threesome, and offered accommodation in a House in the Country. AH! I anticipated, back-to-the-land! But that wasn't quite it. The four of us, with our three cats, crammed ourselves into a tiny suburban ranch-style house. True, we had a fireplace, and a couple of goats next door, but as for free and easy rural living — forget it. The Chief of Police lived up the road and we were scared to death he'd find out what we were *doing* in that house. The major shopping malls were five minutes away. We never even put in a garden.

When the landlord decided to move back in, I determined to give the city one last try. Tired of moving, spoiled by the burbs, it wasn't long after we'd been broken into in our last city flat, that we three, my lover, the original store recruit and I, pooled our meager savings and put a down payment on a townhouse condo near Long Island Sound. Still young, idealistic, touched as I'd been by collectivism and back-to-the-landism, buying a home shook my self-image. Yet here, finally, was a home safe enough, big enough, warm enough; a home where no one could forbid our new cats, block our cars, throw us out for being dykes. Long before Guppies were invented, I'd, half-ashamed, half-proud, become a full-fledged Guppy.

And there I thought it would end. The condo exceeded any housing ambition I'd ever imagined. I was fiercely proud and possessive of it. I could see the water. I had a workroom where I could actually write in privacy. I had miles of shoreline, though not quite the Oregon coast, and safe neighborhoods to walk. Other gays from the Parkway, from the convenience store chain, had begun to move into surrounding condos. I loved it there. I wrote my first book there. At last I had no desire to move on.

But there were other gay geographical trends I hadn't yet lived. My lover wanted to move to the West Coast.

Eight years and many thousands of miles later, after battles and conflicts, changes and changes and changes, I've stopped fighting the West. The West has won me. A client of mine recently described me as the most laid-back person he knows. (I chuckled inside, recalling collective hysteria on House Meeting Nights). Rather than cling for life to home ownership, I let the house I bought with my ex go — back to the sellers.

I keep trying to make life simpler, to hone it down to something that's organically me. Not a generation, not a political movement, not a dependence on purveyors of alcohol. Just a place where the stresses of city life don't beset me and I can live like a penniless Guppy, if there is such a thing, in peace, free of the cycles of getting and spending without any rhetoric about it.

My last trip East horrified me. In cars I fought the impulse to cover my eyes with my arms at the sight and sense of assaultive traffic. My lungs filled up, my throat was sore. My doctor discovered radioactivity in my body. I longed for Oregon, for the cities not yet out of hand and the country not yet condominimized. For my 31' x 8' trailer. I keep feeling like, after only two and a half years, I've no right to call the West my home, but I can't deny the bubbling joy I felt at getting back here.

It may be that my search for home isn't over; that I haven't finished with moving on. But it sure feels an awful lot like home around here. I sure do hope the geography of gay allows this gadabout heart to rest.

National Women's Music Festival

The midwest was a welcome haven from controversy.
Perhaps it was all there, under the surface, and I as a
guest was spared it. In any case I found the women I met
— from New York to Sheboygan Falls, welcoming and
appreciative of all the National Women's Music Festival
had to offer.

For me, music festivals have been damp or hot buggy
treks into a wilderness which distracts from the culture at
hand. But NWMF is held on the University of Indiana

campus at Bloomington. Participants are housed in dorms, performers dance, sing, read, talk, in classrooms, auditoriums, lounges. The main stage is a huge balconied hall with excellent acoustics. Across it went Ferron, Toshi Reagon, Judy Sloan, Ronnie Gilbert, Adrienne Torf, Linda Tillery and Band (especially that dynamic keyboard musician Julie Homi in her short white dress and yellow sneakers), Robin Tyler, June Millington, Alive, Beth York, Casselberry and DuPree, and the Wright Dance Company. At the end of the last performance the festival organizers and crew dramatically ascended on a platform from the orchestra pit for deserved accolades.

I was there for the Writers' Conference, and though writers were not treated with as much panache as the musicians, the conference was well-attended. Ruth Peters, who did an impressively efficient job of organizing cultural events, tells me the goal is to expand the Writers' Conference to the level of the Music Industry Conference which took place just prior to the festival. Future plans include bringing together women authors, editors, press, publishers, etc. for three to four days of intense networking. This, plus a booking period for authors to establish speaking engagements, is a sorely needed event and I am anxious to support it and to see it happen.

Judy Grahn was a featured writer, along with Kate Clinton, who taught comedy writing, and myself. Judy is always an inspiration for me. Looking attractively older and healthier than the thin, intense traveller I first saw read in New Haven fourteen years earlier, she still fills an auditorium with a presence I can only call lesbian divinity. Her Common Woman poems have been published and republished, her *Amazon of Wands* (Crossing) is another major work that changed the course of lesbian literature. I am glad to see her reading public

176

growing as this woman's words are like proud clothing we can don again and again to strut and preen in, reminded of our own worth and beauty. Describing herself as the ceremonial dyke she researched for *Another Mother Tongue; Gay Words, Gay Worlds* (Beacon), Grahn brought proof of our gay and lesbian history and culture to us. Her new poetry, like her old, had me crying, so powerfully moving, so deep inside my lesbian psyche does she touch.

I was part of a panel featuring Toni Armstrong, publisher of *Hot Wire,* the women's music industry magazine. She's a hard-driving professional whose publication reflects that in quality and scope. Jeri Edwards, who published *I Know You Know,* a pioneer glossy lesbian magazine, shared her expertise.

At another workshop Tracy Baim spoke. Small, surprisingly young for her accomplishments, she was associate editor of Chicago's *Gay Life* at the time. She created and edited "Sister Spirit," several pullout pages designed to allow women readers to circumvent the "jockstrap ads." Tracy impressed me as one of a whole new breed of young women willing to unite with men to create a strong gay culture. It makes me wonder, have the older separatists done some healing for us, so the dykes coming up and out can live without so much rancor? Have some gay men achieved such a measure of feminism we can work together with more ease?

The Feminist Writers' Guild is very active in the Chicago-Indianapolis area and there were may Guild members at NWMF. One workshop addressed the need for the group to provide peer support, advice and programs such as health insurance to those of us trying to survive by writing. Once more, it was heartening to see women like Jorjet Harper, the Guild's administrative coordinator, working toward professionalism on their own terms, creating their own structures, meeting their own needs.

Videotaping Judy Grahn and every other performer they could, was JO/ED Video, a team of two women who drive endless miles each year to preserve women's/lesbian herstory. They're building a visual archive they're eager to share and thus far have tapes of, among others, Robin Tyler, Rita Mae Brown, Ginny Clemons, Barbara Grier.

Underlying the success of this festival for me was the Sober Support Series, a twenty-four hour women-only space where meetings of Alcoholics, Narcotics, Overeaters and Emotions Anonymous and Adult Children of Alcoholics were held. Organized by Cindy McCammack, SS was a place with a twelve step structure, where any woman could go for talk, sharing, crying, festival stress syndrome, or addiction problems. I spent hours there, working to keep my sanity in a setting where even non-performers were coping with overload. One of the most important hours for me was just prior to my first appearance in a great big lecture hall all by myself in front of a huge number of strangers with a MICROPHONE. I arrived at the Sober Support lounge paralyzed with fear, mute, and left calmed, reassured, less sick to my stomach, on a carpet of good wishes and understanding.

The festival brought together an enormous and eclectic variety of women's energy. At a reception, the Writers' Conference merged momentarily with the concurrent Spirituality Conference. Autographing books were Z Budapest, striking in her flowing clothing; Diane Mariechild, soft, likeable author of *Mother Wit,* and Merlin Stone, art herstorian as well as author of *Ancient Mirrors of Womanhood.*

We mingled with autograph seekers in a room which also held the visual arts exhibit. It was dizzying to talk to

Yvonne Zipter, poet, columnist and organizer of the Writers' Conference; look up to see all that moving visual art; buy books by Judy, Diane, Merlin, from Indianapolis' Dreams and Swords Bookstore owner Harriet Clare (who really knows how to sell books); and move on to a performance by Portland's own Dyketones — that's the kind of vision, maturity and respect for one another's efforts, as well as allowance for one another's mistakes that's creating room for us to grow too strong to be put down. Too strong to be silenced ever again.

Southern Route

My main impressions from a quick Southern tour are vociferous songbirds and consistently lovely women. One friend reminded me that Southern women have a reputation for physical beauty, but I'd never thought that conventional good looks might transfer to our own. Secondary impression: Stately buildings surrounded by blazing azaleas, long quiet blocks of porch-fronted homes in both black and white neighborhoods, and rooms full of laughing, applauding, culture-hungry women.

Norfolk, Virginia, is a Navy town; flat and unpretty except for the waterfront. There, a festive shopping mall is backed by older shops and fronted by a view of the most enormous ships I have ever seen. Pretty scary.

But Dr. Ellen Lewin, Director of Women's Studies at a local school, wasn't scary at all. We went to high school together twenty-six years ago. I admired her enormously. She was a fifteen-year-old radical before the age of radicals. Today (after reconnecting through my books last year) she thinks she's mellowed, but obviously forgets that the field of women's studies is a tenuous cutting edge through society's misconceptions, preconceptions and preoccupation with conception — and that the teachers are the vulnerable blades.

Ellen brought me together with a small and brave group of women who have formed the Tidewater Bookshelf, a bookstore without a home which travels to its customers with lesbian and feminist titles. They dared not advertise too blatantly — many of the women involved are Naval personnel. Others are simply Southerners with a healthy respect for one tradition of their homeland: eradication of queers. Not that the South is any different from anyplace else. It just seems to be more so. But then, my audience was more so, too — one of the most appreciative I've ever had. The attorney who'd just started practice, the Naval officers who'd enlisted for training they never got, the writer who'd heard that publishing with a lesbian press was the kiss of death. I reminded her of Isabel Miller, Judy Grahn and Rita Mae Brown.

On the way to Richmond, Ellen took me strolling through Williamsburg, a reconstruction of a colonial town. Though real people live in the real houses, tourist groups ran amok and there were few signs of real history: pigs slopping in the mud, slaves struggling survive, fragrant outdoor plumbing. And we complain that the Soviet Union rewrites history!

Lesbians, however, are similar everywhere. Representatives from the local softball team — "Soft Touch" — were on hand to cheer my softball story. They had a story of their own: of their one-armed teammate who can catch a ball and have it back in the air again in the blink of an eye.

Helen Whiting of the Regulator Bookstore squired me around Durham, N.C. She was one of several military daughters I met who opted to settle in the South. I stayed with Kristen, retail manager of Ladyslipper, a national woman's music distributor and mail order company. Her large breezy home is in an impressively integrated neighborhood.

Readings at The Regulator are very Southern. I felt as if I was presiding over an at-home tea as I sat on a wrap-around cushioned bench with my visitors. One woman had driven a great distance with her three young sons and their just-weaned kittens. While the boys stayed outside looking for kitten homes, mom listened to old-dyke-tales-by-request. I was gratified by Durham's yen for my characters. More than Western or Northeastern readers, the woman of the South seemed to fall in love with fictional characters and have an endless curiosity about their ongoing lives.

A New Yorker drove me down to Greensboro, North Carolina. Her non-drawl was like a breath of home. But in Greensboro I was plunged once more into musical voices: Kim, assistant manager of White Rabbit Books, which is owned by John Neil, greeted me, along with Cathy, a filmmaker who, with backing and time, plans to rival

Donna Deitch's *Desert Hearts*. Jody was there, too, a jewelry-maker who wends her way down from the mountains of North Carolina to spend her weekends in the gay community. Greensboro, like the other cities I visited, may not boast of its gay people, but there are four bars in the small city. Two of them have drag shows — a well-entrenched Southern tradition enjoyed by lesbians right along with gay men.

I stayed with Kathy and Karen, who are members of Lesbians Up For New Adventures (LUNA), which co-sponsored, with White Rabbit, my trip. Both women are Virgos like myself. It has been my observation that Virgos have difficulty, to say the least, in making decisions together, in out-courtesying one another, and in penetrating one another's stubbornness. Our threesome proved me right. Once the initial, and riotous, negotiations were over, I rested until it was time to travel to a Unitarian church in the woods where women overflowed the seats to hear excerpts from *Dusty's Queen of Hearts Diner*.

Besides the Virgos, songbirds and lesbian beauty, the other commonality I found was a scarcity of gay writers visiting the South. The women were *so* glad to see me in person, and seemed so stimulated by what I read, that I wonder if alliances can be made between booksellers and grassroots groups in the various cities to establish a Southern Route on the Amazon Trail. Once formed, such a network could also supplement any in place to fight censorship and obscenity laws. In Durham I declined to read erotica because a gentleman in business attire, clean-shaven, bellied, stood nearby staring blank-faced into a single book throughout most of my reading. In Greensboro, after the reading, Karen mentioned that I could have been arrested for reading a story called "Dusty

Eats Out"' thought she assured me there'd been no police in the audience. As I write this at Chicago's O'Hare International, I'm aware of breathing a little bit easier. From those big destroyers (literally) in Norfolk, to those little words in state statutes that restrict the freedom of speech and the right to life, liberty and the pursuit of happiness embodied in Williamsburg, I was more aware than usual of the risks a lesbian takes to write about her life.

When it was over, when my last words hung naked and vulnerable in the balmy North Carolina air, Kathy and Karen whisked me off to a "pasture party" given by a couple who own a local stable. It was a comforting sight. At least two hundred lesbians, along with a handful of gay men, talked and danced around a huge bonfire which glowed orange and bright. I watched older femmes, baby butches, dancing boys; smelled horses, burning wood; heard rock music by the pond, and the shouts and laughter of a people set free, for a few hours, to love one another in the open, before the flickering bonfire light, under the dark and — unfortunately for the revelers — not always gracious Southern sky.

San Francisco Stories

My mini-tour began at San Francisco Airport when the Mission-Castro Super Shuttle bus arrived. It was propelled by a punky young dyke with yellow hair and emphatic dark eyebrows. She grinned and ushered me into the front seat beside her — just 'cause I was a dyke, too.

The editor of *Feminist Bookstore News*, Carol Seajay, a writer herself whose work appears in *A Faith of One's Own* among other places, greeted me at her Mission doorstep along with her cat Chia, and we got right down to business: Talking lesbian books till the wee small hours. Carol's apartment, decorated with a treasure trove of review copies of books, looks out on a warren of urban backyards, crisscrossing staircases and porches. One neighbor had dressed a tree in necklaces and such. Many of the other neighbors were feline, and the cat-caphony they raised echoed up the wall at odd hours, a city song.

The alleyway also houses a large and vocal first, second and third generation immigrant family. The second generation son was in prison for a while. On his return he rented a garage in Carol's building and began an auto repair business. Neighborhood teenage boys, who until then had amused themselves with vandalizing buildings, flocked to this unofficial training center and went to work on cars. The vandals became competent mechanics. The graffiti and other damage stopped.

When a new landlord bought the building, the mechanic couldn't afford the hiked rent. He sadly prepared to move away from his neighborhood and his trainees. But unseen forces, in the guise of Miz Seajay, a dyke with a wise heart, whispered in the owner's ear: wouldn't it be smarter, safer, to keep the garage rent, and the vandalism repair bills, low, by letting the shop stay? The mechanic asked Carol a few days later, "Was it you who put in the good word for us?"

It wasn't long after this that a new lesbian was moving into the building. The vandal-trainees were hanging around the garage. One of them greeted the woman and her retinue of butchy moving-day helpers with groans of, "Not another damn dyke!" and the like. It didn't take long, though, for what went around, to come around.

The mechanic whispered into the trainees' ears. While the actual taunter hung behind, a couple of others, gruffly bashful, went up to the new woman. "Aw," they told her, "he was just in a bad mood. Don't lissen to 'im." They thereupon grabbed the heaviest items and, macho, lugged them upstairs side by side with the dyke's butchy friends.

Stories. Everywhere stories. I went to read at Mama Bears in Oakland, a half-bookstore, half performance space-restaurant. Alice Malloy, intense and fascinating with her own stories of her Lower East Side New York old gay self, welcomed me and my escorts Carol and Cheryl. I had remembered Cheryl as painfully shy, but the woman I hung out with that night was charming and terribly sweet. She works with bag ladies and is said to be amazingly effective with them. Street people, so shy of the world. Cheryl, finding a way out of shyness.

Nor was she the only one. Two women in the audience that night had been at the West Coast Festival last summer. One of them, her lover had explained then, had been too shy to ask me to sign a book, so the lover had asked for her. Five months later, not only did they show up at Mama Bears to hear me read again, but the shy woman came up to me *herself* this time! I was thrilled.

Jennifer and Tiana welcomed me to Old Wives Tales the next night. The crowd was larger and just as warm. I kept having flashes of a June night in 1982, my first trip to the West Coast, when Barbara Grier spoke at Old Wives Tales. She introduced many women in the room, including me, all a-twitter, the about-to-become-a-published-author. The highlight of the evening was Barbara's introduction of a pretty middle-aged linguistics teacher in a pants suit who just happened to have written the Beebo Brinker books which I'd come out on twenty-two years earlier: Ann Bannon. How we all cheered! And here I was, four books behind me, a real live author at Old Wives Tales at last.

That same night in '82 at Artemis Cafe I'd learned that writers don't just get to think up stories in their safe, cozy lairs. Donna McBride of Naiad Press just kind of casually mentioned that real live authors did readings. I almost choked on my bagel. Read? Aloud? To rooms full of real live *people*? (Cats, maybe.) Talk about painfully shy. Talk about a sudden need to find a way out of shyness. I was physically ill for every one of my first dozen or so readings. But I love them (mostly) now.

Love them for the people I met at Clairelight Books in Santa Rosa: Enthusiastic, laughing, responsive. Claire herself is all a bookseller should be, a bright beaming beacon greeting authors and audience alike with the same fervor.

It was Ardy who whisked me away the next day, from the shopping center where Clairelight is flanked by a maternity shop and a beauty parlor, to Lioness Books in Sacramento. Ardy and I swapped old gay stories all the way there. And discovered with great excitement that she used to hang out at the same bars in LA as Benita Kirkland, author of *Death Strip* — if Ms. Kirkland, who did work the LA burlesque houses, used the name Midnight.

There's one more story I want to tell from my mini-tour. One more time when I free-fell, alone in a strange city, into the arms of the gay community and found myself right at home.

While still in San Francisco I decided to replace my twenty-four year old flight jacket. I'd been to Ollie's bar in Oakland the night before to visit with Ollie and her lover, Nadine. I'd felt not a little shabby under the various battle-scars and shredding fabrics of my beloved coat. After all, how often do I get to a gay bar these days? Especially the bar which comes closest to my ideal, *Cafe Femmes*. I think it was Ollie who teased me about my disintegrating jacket. I suppose until then I'd thought clothing so old and comfortable must be invisible, or have so much character it commanded admiration.

Jefferson, a character in my stories, wears a cracked and faded brown leather bomber jacket. Ever since I first imagined the jacket, I'd wanted it. My royalty check was on its way and I always try to treat myself from royalties as a reward for working my ass off all year.

Carol Seajay took me over to the Haight where we raided the Aardvark, a used clothing store. There, displayed high on a wall, was a $200 jacket that looked just like Jefferson's. But $200 was too big a chunk of my anticipated check. A saleswoman, long-skirted-and-haired, high-booted and earringed (in other words, whom I'd assume was straight) sympathetically suggested I try two gay male leather stores on Polk Street. Carol had an appointment in the opposite direction, so I bumbled myself onto a couple of wrong buses and eventually got downtown to the Polk Street bus stop. There I had to face the task, without street numbers, of asking someone *where* on Polk the leather shops might be.

I sidled up to a man whom I strongly suspected would be familiar with such information. I cleared my throat, "Do you know where Wendell's Leather store is on Polk?" I asked.

His manner reassured me, but when he couldn't identify the cross street I needed I plunged on. Then I, always a lesbian, in the past a separatist, also still partly a nice-girl-from-Queens, cleared my throat again and asked,

"How about, ah-hem, uh — 'Hard On Leathers'?" I *really* wanted this jacket.

Straight-faced, he promised to tell me where to disembark and we began to talk as we waited. I mentioned living near Grants Pass.

"Grants Pass!" Patrick exclaimed, fluttering with excitement. He named the small town where I live nearby.

"Who do you know *there*?" I asked, excited myself.

It turned out that his brother is our nearest gay neighbor and a good friend who'd been to dinner just a few weeks before. Patrick and I practically danced onto the bus, chattering and smiling all the way to You-Know-What Leathers. We arranged to get together again in Oregon, and parted full of the wonder of discovering once more that everyone in the gay community is related at least once to everyone else.

With a sign like my chance meeting with Patrick, of course I found Jefferson's Jacket, perfectly cracked, faded, and affordable, at Wendell's. Not only that, but to the collection of stories I'd bring back along the Amazon Trail I could add another: How I'd picked up a gay man in San Francisco!

Seattle: A Land of New Beginnings

When I heard that Jane Rule would be giving a workshop at the University of Washington in Seattle, I felt my heart hitch itself to a wagon of unstoppable hopes. I didn't know why I had to get there, 400 miles from my home, to a city I'd never been in, but I was on my way before I could stop to figure it out.

Sensibly, I'd planned to drive 'til dark, then stop at a motel. But as it happened, the sky lingered lavender like some muse-lit beacon, until I was so close to Seattle I just kept on. If I was surprised to find the I-5 corridor through Washington to be littered with urban and suburban growths, I was shocked by the monstrosity of Seattle, a city I'd heard was beautiful, but which seemed hardly that as I cruised in under the massive steel and concrete loops of a super highway.

Yet I had a great time that next day, before the University of Washington began its program of panels and readings by Northwest women. I hopped a bus first thing in the morning and got a closet tour guide for a driver. She plied me with so much must-see information that I veered from my planned route of Gay highlights to take in the Pike Place Market, a rambling bayside fun-house of shops and stalls.

Feeling I'd done my duty, I legged it toward our part of town, putting something like eight miles on my Sauconys before I was done that day.

First stop: Beyond the Closet, a bookshop operated by Ron Whiteaker, former manager of A Different Light Bookstore in L.A. On the corner of Pike, *the* Gay street, and Belmont, on Capitol Hill, *the* Gay neighborhood, Ron's got a light and airy literary sanctuary which feels as welcoming as any I've been in. Gertrude the zany kitten seems to assist him by entertaining dykes like me.

While I was with Ron, a man rushed into the store, threw the door shut and locked it, then pressed himself flat against a wall. "I'm being followed by a madman!" he said in a terrified whisper. Sure enough, his pursuer stopped at the plate glass windows and glared in. The incident was small, but apropos. Beyond the Closet really was a sanctuary for this causal customer. On the other hand, the very statement of openness produced by the large windows, the good lighting, the central location, made both the pursued, and his champion, sitting ducks. I appreciated as never before the risks gentle Ron Whiteaker and all his counterparts take daily to keep Gay culture, and in more than one sense, Gay people, alive.

I scouted Pike Street, reported that the coast was clear, then pressed on.

Seattle Gay News was next, where the staff was birthing a new issue of this increasingly hefty paper. Then all along Pike came the bars, mostly men's. Next door to the tattoo parlor was one of the nicest Lesbian bars I've ever been in. It was absolutely thrilled to be greeted by a smiling waitperson. I was even more thrilled when I could sit at the bar like a big old-time butch — and order nothing more addictive than lunch.

Even after I left "The Hill" I was not alone. Seal Press is in Seattle. Katie Niles, the photographer, has moved there. The city has its own commercial association and I clutched its guide to Gay businesses as I went. A mainstream bookstore on Broadway has shelves and shelves devoted to us. The Red and the Black, an alternative bookshop, had even more. All over the city, as a matter of fact, I found blatant signs of our pervasive rooting.

A friend who lives in San Francisco explained it. "Everyone's moving to Seattle," she said simply. Several folks I met in Seattle agreed. "People want to get away from the AIDS thing as much as they can."

Indeed, with all the construction going on, and the city is notorious for its recent building, Seattle felt like a land of new beginnings. As I walked through one section of the city, my attention was suddenly caught by an incredible ski jump view of the Space Needle, floating in a mist off in the distance. I hadn't noticed the Seattle hills before. The blanched light. The trendy if not trend-setting shops. The sections of the city with personalities almost as distinctive

193

as Russian Hill or The Mission. And of course that west coast openness, mellowness, was as prevalent as Birkenstocks and Stash tea. Is the attraction of Seattle that it is *almost* San Francisco?

Footsore, a bit disoriented, I spent the rest of the weekend in the University neighborhood getting exactly what I needed: a renewed sense of myself as a writer. I had no illusions that I belonged in this community of academic authors. For the most part I felt like a sore thumb amongst the feminist literati, though I enjoyed much of their work and loved seeing a program of women writers. At the same time, I felt safe in Seattle from the temptation of commercial fiction, which I seem incapable of mastering in any case. Despite a great and perhaps desperate desire to toss my schizophrenia-inducing straight job into Puget Sound, fast-paced plots and cliff-hanger action, which are the way to make money with the written word these days, elude my earnest and struggling characters.

Jane Rule, though she is honored in both the academic and commercial spheres, transcends both. *Desert of the Heart,* first published in 1964, dared to speak positively about Lesbians. And spoke about us, not in lurid language, but in a literate style no self-respecting commercial publisher — who published books about dykes — would normally touch. As in all of her work, Rule created a world in which moral dilemmas engage the characters, with the end result that love in any form is never successfully rejected. She writes from, and about, the heart.

I needed to be reminded that the heart is where I must settle too. I've fled into some sanctuaries, terrified of what I'd found while exploring. I've tried *almost* cities, (like living through chemicals) where life seemed easier than

194

the mean streets of my own soul. Now I felt lost in a tangle of steel and concrete loops (paths cut for others), that left me uncertain of my direction.

It wasn't so much what Jane Rule said, although all of it helped, it was more that her solid physical presence, the stories she told of her life, repeated what I'd learned from her books. And what I'd learned was terribly simple. I wanted to spend my life doing what Rule does so well: to write from my heart in a way that will enhance the lives of my readers. It was worth the trip.

Marching Home

I hadn't been to a Gay Pride March in six years, which I now know is a mistake, and I hadn't been able to attend the March on Washington in the fall of 1987. I was determined to do what I could to swell the ranks of some March somewhere.

Around the same time that I made this decision I also was coming to realize that after four years of living in Oregon, and eighteen before that of living in Connecticut, I still thought of New York City as my home. I had no

196

intention of living there again, and this year would not even set foot closer than an airport. Wasn't it about time that I settle, in both senses of the word, on a place of my own?

I could not bring myself to adopt Southern Oregon as home. It's too hard to be queer here. Impossible to be openly queer. On the other hand, I am not about to move away from Girlfriend, nor am I willing to abandon some of the loveliest territory in the universe to fundamentalist Christians, conservative survivalists and macho methamphetamine manufacturers.

I was scheduled to attend San Francisco's Living Sober gathering again this year. It is, like their Gay Pride Parade, one of the largest in the country and my experiences at both had been gratifying, if a bit overwhelming. It struck me, though, that this running to the major events in the major cities where the major celebrities spoke was not going to help me take root. Maybe I should consider making my statements where I live.

The first time I visited Portland, Oregon, I was not, to say the least, impressed. It was little (population 366,383), it was inland, it was for the most part flat and had no Castro, no Stonewall, no Mardigras or cobblestones or gay literary history. It did have one tall building. Big fat hairy deal, as Garfield would say.

Yet Portland's *Just Out*, highly regarded by the gay press industry, has loyally run this column for over three years. And Portland's A Woman's Place Bookstore is one of the oldest in the country.

What's more, the state is filled with maverick women and men whom I admire enormously. Billy Russo of Roseburg quit his secure federal job, cashed in his retirement and created Ruby House, an AIDS Hospice in a rural redneck town of 16,000. The state is famous for its women's land groups: Owl Farm in Days Creek, Womanshare in Grants Pass, Rainbow's End in Roseburg, to name a few. The radical faeries meet annually on Creek Land, five miles north of where I live. Womanspirit Magazine lived its potent life here and this was the birthplace of RFD, the magazine for rural gay men.

Southern Oregon is also one of the few temperate places in America where I can make enough to live on a part-time job so that I can write. This nesting process, I came to realize, had to do with accepting who I was, what I needed and what my life had become.

So I made my decision. I would march as close to home as possible, in Portland. And I would celebrate my sobriety at Soberfaire, a weekend of meetings and workshops in Portland. I would settle for Oregon to see if I could settle in it.

Soberfaire was just what I needed. It was held in a neighborhood full of graceful older apartment buildings, trees, a commercial strip where the gay and lesbian film festival was blatantly advertised on a marquee. I suppose there were between 200 and 250 people at Soberfaire. I remember that most of the workshops I attended at Living Sober in San Francisco had been so large there had been a charismatic quality to them. A leader or a well-spoken participant would move the room to emotional heights until I felt as if each session had been highly cathartic, revelatory, life-changing. It was what I'd needed then.

In Portland, the groups were small. Not only did I, Mizz Bashful, feel a responsibility to contribute by opening my mouth and sharing, but I felt comfortable enough to do so. No one walked around hugging teddy bears. I didn't feel as if I needed to. Soberfaire for me was not so much about moving to new places in sobriety as recognizing where I am.

One realization that came out of Soberfaire for me was about anger. I'd spent a lot of time fuming about the people who were organizing against gays in my small town. I'd gotten a little obsessive about it. Was beginning to feel consumed by my anger. When I talked about this at Soberfaire one group leader, also an alcoholism counselor, told a story about how she realized that she could not live in the small town where she had grown up. She loved it, but it was like mine, bigoted and ignorant. Her message, clearly, was that I had choices. I could move.

Well, I was there because I'd decided *not* to move. So I got angry at the group leader. Which I knew was silly. Maybe my problem was not the bigots, but the anger itself. Maybe the anger didn't have a whole lot to do with the bigots. Maybe if I could separate my anger from that issue, then the actions I was taking because of it, to use up the angry energy, would finally be able to do just that.

The next weekend I traveled to Portland again for the March. It was one of the actions I'd planned to take to turn my anger to good. I'd seen the anti-gay demonstrators back in my town during the week and been infuriated even further. They'd set up a fortress outside the Post Office: a round table with a beach umbrella to shade them from the searing Oregon sun. I was ready to march.

I kept remembering what I'd realized the week before, though, and had spent some time identifying the source of my anger, which went way back to New York, my beloved home town. I'd drawn a picture of part of that anger. Of a thirteen-year-old tomboy striding past the city playground, and of the teenagers on the other side of the

199

chainlink fence yelling, "Hey, butch!" at this kid who didn't even know what the word meant. "Is it a boy?" they sang every time I went by, "or is it a girl?" I wanted to run, I wanted to kill, I wanted to hide somewhere and never come out again.

I marched by them, helplessly swallowing my anger. Who could I tell? It was true. I didn't look like the other girls. My mother complained about it all the time. What could I do? I was a gay child in a hostile straight world which was full of boys shouting insults.

I marched by the teenagers again in Portland, but I was marching alongside a lot of tomboys, blocks and blocks of tomboys and sissies and butches and drag queens. The anger was there, but it had finished its job for now: it had driven me home and it was tempered with relief and with joy.

A few of the publications of
THE NAIAD PRESS, INC.
P.O. Box 10543 ● **Tallahassee, Florida 32302**
Phone (904) 539-9322
Mail orders welcome. Please include 15% postage.

THE AMAZON TRAIL by Lee Lynch. 216 pp. Life, travel & lore of famous lesbian author. ISBN 0-941483-27-4 $8.95

THE FINER GRAIN by Denise Ohio. 216 pp. Brilliant young college lesbian novel. ISBN 0-941483-11-8   8.95

HIGH CONTRAST by Jessie Lattimore. 264 pp. Women of the Crystal Palace. ISBN 0-941483-17-7   8.95

OCTOBER OBSESSION by Meredith More. Josie's rich, secret Lesbian life. ISBN 0-941483-18-5   8.95

LESBIAN CROSSROADS by Ruth Baetz. 276 pp. Contemporary Lesbian lives. ISBN 0-941483-21-5   9.95

BEFORE STONEWALL: THE MAKING OF A GAY AND LESBIAN COMMUNITY by Andrea Weiss & Greta Schiller. 96 pp., 25 illus. ISBN 0-941483-20-7   7.95

WE WALK THE BACK OF THE TIGER by Patricia A. Murphy. 192 pp. Romantic Lesbian novel/beginning women's movement.
ISBN 0-941483-13-4   8.95

SUNDAY'S CHILD by Joyce Bright. 216 pp. Lesbian athletics, at last the novel about sports. ISBN 0-941483-12-6   8.95

OSTEN'S BAY by Zenobia N. Vole. 204 pp. Sizzling adventure romance set on Bonaire. ISBN 0-941483-15-0   8.95

LESSONS IN MURDER by Claire McNab. 216 pp. 1st in a stylish mystery series. ISBN 0-941483-14-2   8.95

YELLOWTHROAT by Penny Hayes. 240 pp. Margarita, bandit, kidnaps Julia. ISBN 0-941483-10-X   8.95

SAPPHISTRY: THE BOOK OF LESBIAN SEXUALITY by Pat Califia. 3d edition, revised. 208 pp. ISBN 0-941483-24-X   8.95

CHERISHED LOVE by Evelyn Kennedy. 192 pp. Erotic Lesbian love story. ISBN 0-941483-08-8   8.95

LAST SEPTEMBER by Helen R. Hull. 208 pp. Six stories & a glorious novella. ISBN 0-941483-09-6   8.95

THE SECRET IN THE BIRD by Camarin Grae. 312 pp. Striking, psychological suspense novel. ISBN 0-941483-05-3   8.95

TO THE LIGHTNING by Catherine Ennis. 208 pp. Romantic Lesbian 'Robinson Crusoe' adventure. ISBN 0-941483-06-1   8.95

AMATEUR CITY by Katherine V. Forrest. 224 pp. A Kate Delafield mystery. First in a series. ISBN 0-930044-55-X 7.95

THE SOPHIE HOROWITZ STORY by Sarah Schulman. 176 pp. Engaging novel of madcap intrigue. ISBN 0-930044-54-1 7.95

THE BURNTON WIDOWS by Vickie P. McConnell. 272 pp. A Nyla Wade mystery, second in the series. ISBN 0-930044-52-5 7.95

OLD DYKE TALES by Lee Lynch. 224 pp. Extraordinary stories of our diverse Lesbian lives. ISBN 0-930044-51-7 8.95

DAUGHTERS OF A CORAL DAWN by Katherine V. Forrest. 240 pp. Novel set in a Lesbian new world. ISBN 0-930044-50-9 7.95

THE PRICE OF SALT by Claire Morgan. 288 pp. A milestone novel, a beloved classic. ISBN 0-930044-49-5 8.95

AGAINST THE SEASON by Jane Rule. 224 pp. Luminous, complex novel of interrelationships. ISBN 0-930044-48-7 8.95

LOVERS IN THE PRESENT AFTERNOON by Kathleen Fleming. 288 pp. A novel about recovery and growth.
ISBN 0-930044-46-0 8.95

TOOTHPICK HOUSE by Lee Lynch. 264 pp. Love between two Lesbians of different classes. ISBN 0-930044-45-2 7.95

MADAME AURORA by Sarah Aldridge. 256 pp. Historical novel featuring a charismatic "seer." ISBN 0-930044-44-4 7.95

CURIOUS WINE by Katherine V. Forrest. 176 pp. Passionate Lesbian love story, a best-seller. ISBN 0-930044-43-6 8.95

BLACK LESBIAN IN WHITE AMERICA by Anita Cornwell. 141 pp. Stories, essays, autobiography. ISBN 0-930044-41-X 7.50

CONTRACT WITH THE WORLD by Jane Rule. 340 pp. Powerful, panoramic novel of gay life. ISBN 0-930044-28-2 7.95

YANTRAS OF WOMANLOVE by Tee A. Corinne. 64 pp. Photos by noted Lesbian photographer. ISBN 0-930044-30-4 6.95

MRS. PORTER'S LETTER by Vicki P. McConnell. 224 pp. The first Nyla Wade mystery. ISBN 0-930044-29-0 7.95

TO THE CLEVELAND STATION by Carol Anne Douglas. 192 pp. Interracial Lesbian love story. ISBN 0-930044-27-4 6.95

THE NESTING PLACE by Sarah Aldridge. 224 pp. A three-woman triangle—love conquers all! ISBN 0-930044-26-6 7.95

THIS IS NOT FOR YOU by Jane Rule. 284 pp. A letter to a beloved is also an intricate novel. ISBN 0-930044-25-8 8.95

FAULTLINE by Sheila Ortiz Taylor. 140 pp. Warm, funny, literate story of a startling family. ISBN 0-930044-24-X 6.95

THE LESBIAN IN LITERATURE by Barbara Grier. 3d ed. Foreword by Maida Tilchen. 240 pp. Comprehensive bibliography. Literary ratings; rare photos. ISBN 0-930044-23-1 7.95

ANNA'S COUNTRY by Elizabeth Lang. 208 pp. A woman
finds her Lesbian identity.   ISBN 0-930044-19-3   6.95

PRISM by Valerie Taylor. 158 pp. A love affair between two
women in their sixties.   ISBN 0-930044-18-5   6.95

BLACK LESBIANS: AN ANNOTATED BIBLIOGRAPHY
compiled by J. R. Roberts. Foreword by Barbara Smith. 112 pp.
Award-winning bibliography.   ISBN 0-930044-21-5   5.95

THE MARQUISE AND THE NOVICE by Victoria Ramstetter.
108 pp. A Lesbian Gothic novel.   ISBN 0-930044-16-9   4.95

OUTLANDER by Jane Rule. 207 pp. Short stories and essays
by one of our finest writers.   ISBN 0-930044-17-7   6.95

ALL TRUE LOVERS by Sarah Aldridge. 292 pp. Romantic
novel set in the 1930s and 1940s.   ISBN 0-930044-10-X   7.95

A WOMAN APPEARED TO ME by Renee Vivien. 65 pp. A
classic; translated by Jeannette H. Foster. ISBN 0-930044-06-1   5.00

CYTHEREA'S BREATH by Sarah Aldridge. 240 pp. Romantic
novel about women's entrance into medicine.
                                             ISBN 0-930044-02-9   6.95

TOTTIE by Sarah Aldridge. 181 pp. Lesbian romance in the
turmoil of the sixties.   ISBN 0-930044-01-0   6.95

THE LATECOMER by Sarah Aldridge. 107 pp. A delicate love
story.   ISBN 0-930044-00-2   5.00

ODD GIRL OUT by Ann Bannon.   ISBN 0-930044-83-5   5.95

I AM A WOMAN by Ann Bannon.   ISBN 0-930044-84-3   5.95

WOMEN IN THE SHADOWS by Ann Bannon.
                                             ISBN 0-930044-85-1   5.95

JOURNEY TO A WOMAN by Ann Bannon.
                                             ISBN 0-930044-86-X   5.95

BEEBO BRINKER by Ann Bannon.   ISBN 0-930044-87-8   5.95
            Legendary novels written in the fifties and sixties,
                 set in the gay mecca of Greenwich Village.

VOLUTE BOOKS

JOURNEY TO FULFILLMENT	Early classics by Valerie	3.95
A WORLD WITHOUT MEN	Taylor: The Erika Frohmann	3.95
RETURN TO LESBOS	series.	3.95

These are just a few of the many Naiad Press titles — we are the oldest and
largest lesbian/feminist publishing company in the world. Please request a
complete catalog. We offer personal service; we encourage and welcome
direct mail orders from individuals who have limited access to bookstores
carrying our publications.